# HOTEL FRONT OFFICE
# SIMULATION

# HOTEL FRONT OFFICE SIMULATION

## SIMULATION

**A WORKBOOK AND SOFTWARE PACKAGE**

SHERYL FRIED KLINE AND WILLIAM SULLIVAN

**John Wiley & Sons, Inc.**

*Library of Congress Cataloging-in-Publication Data:*

Fried-Kline, Sheryl.
   Hotel front office simulation : a workbook and software package /
Sheryl Fried Kline and William Sullivan.
       p. cm.
     ISBN 0-471-20331-9 (acid-free paper)
   1. Hotel front desk personnel—Handbooks, manuals, etc.  2. Hotel
management—Handbooks, manuals, etc.  I. Sullivan, William.  II. Title.
     TX911.3.F75 F75 2002
     647.94'068'3—dc21

                                                    2002001010

Printed in the United States of America

10 9 8 7 6 5 4 3 2 1

# CONTENTS

# INTRODUCTION

This software program and student workbook provide you with a simulation of a hotel front office experience. The software is, at its core, a 25-room hotel called the Sullklin Inn. You will use an actual hotel property management system used by hundreds of hotels. The program is adapted from Innstar, a software package developed by Visual One Systems.

The software and workbook are designed for a curriculum that covers topics related to hotel management and hotel front office operations. It can accompany a variety of front office management textbooks or stand alone. This package is designed for use in a classroom laboratory setting or by an individual student in a self-paced environment. It is written from the point of view of someone with little or no hotel front office experience. That said, the software should be familiar to those individuals who have worked at a front desk and have used any other property management system (PMS).

The workbook guides you through the guest cycle from the reservation process to the night audit. Registration, posting, and guest service functions are covered in detail. The system also covers issues relating to the housekeeping, PBX, and maintenance departments. Each chapter takes you step by step through each aspect of the guest cycle. Exercises at the end of each chapter are designed to let you practice what you have just learned.

**Chapter 1** describes how to use the software and workbook. The basics for using this software, which is easy to use and keyboard-driven, are covered in detail. You will quickly learn to navigate the software from opening the program to logging off. This chapter also describes the fictional hotel property, the Sullklin Inn.

**Chapter 2** describes the reservation process. You are guided through the creation of a variety of reservations and are given the chance to explore special reservation situations. You will use both the individual and group reservation modules. The reservation process includes changing and canceling reservations, creating group reservations, and picking up rooms from group blocks. You are also introduced to several reservation reports in this chapter. Finally, room availability and daily summary screens are analyzed in this chapter.

**Chapter 3** is all about the registration process. You will learn to check in guests as walk-ins and those with reservations. Each step in the registration process is discussed from the moment the guest arrives at the hotel until he or she is given a room number and directed to a room. Several special situations are also discussed. You will select rooms based upon room type and location. As you would find in an actual hotel, the Sullklin Inn has three room types: king bed, double-double, and suite. Rooms offer views of the pool or park and are available in smoking and nonsmoking options.

**Chapter 4** covers posting and folio management. The cashier functions include posting a variety of payments and charges. Debits and credits and the posting function of this PMS are also explored in this chapter. You will learn to make posting corrections and transfer charges, as well as the steps in a check-out process; finally, you'll learn how to generate the cashier-end-of shift report.

**Chapter 5** involves two important hotel departments—housekeeping and maintenance—and describes how they interface with the front desk. These two functions are used in this chapter to demonstrate their impact on the operation of the front desk. The telephone department and PBX functions are also explored. You will learn how to change room status and housekeeping conditions for hotel rooms. You'll also learn how to handle maintenance work orders and telephone messages.

**Chapter 6,** the last chapter, details how to run a full night audit. The reports generated by the night audit are discussed in detail. You will learn how to read the reports and gain a basic understanding of the steps involved in doing the night audit. As examples, room charges and room taxes are posted during this process. You'll discover that at the end of the night audit, the system date changes, and why this is important to the operation of the system.

Innstar is an interactive software program—meaning that, as you enter data, the hotel's occupancy status changes and room availability updates—therefore, you learn as if you were using a real property management system, but in an educational setting. In short, you have the simulated experience of working one day in the life of a 25-room hotel; you will learn by doing.

So congratulations! You can think of yourself as having just purchased your own 25-room hotel. Go to the first chapter to begin your hotel management learning adventure.

# SUPPLEMENTARY MATERIALS

An *Instructor's Manual* (0-471-20777-2) accompanies this workbook and software package. The *Instructor's Manual* contains additional exercises, answers to the workbook exercises, and transparency masters. Related PowerPoint Presentations are available on the companion Web site, www.wiley.com/college.

# ACKNOWLEDGMENTS

I thank my partner in this project and great friend, Professor Sheryl Kline, for her patience and professionalism throughout this challenging project. This book would not have happened without her ideas and the determination that she exhibits every day. Thanks also to our technical partners, who provided the software and technical advice: David Burroughs, President of Visual One Systems, and Eli Nadel, Vice President of Technology, both offered outstanding support for this effort and helped institute the process to make this software available for our students' use. David has always led the industry in his dedication to education, specifically in ensuring that faculty have access to the software in the classroom so that students may gain hands-on learning experiences.

I also want to thank the three most important people in my life: my daughters, Lauren, Kathleen, and Christine. My love for them inspires me to create and teach and do the things that make life worth living.

Bill Sullivan
Widener University
University of Delaware

I thank my colleague and friend, Bill Sullivan, for his patience, vision, and expertise.  He is one of the rare leaders in the hospitality industry who generously give of their time and knowledge to improve the industry as a whole. It was a great privilege to work with him on this project.

There are many people at Widener University I also want to thank: Dean Nicholas Hadgis for his career guidance and constant support; acting President Larry Buck, and the Faculty Sabbatical Committee, which granted the sabbatical that gave me the time to devote to this project; Professor Connie Holt, for her friendship and outstanding persuasive abilities. In addition, the staff at the Information Technology Department at Widener answered many questions and provided technical support. Thanks also to Nancy Keating for her patience and computer skills.

Several students who beta-tested earlier versions of this program deserve thanks for their excellent feedback: Kristin Badiali, Kimberly Bryan, Fernando Polanco, Eric Dunn, and Debbie Sulecki. Thanks also to students, past, present, and future. Their curiosity, energy, and eagerness to learn drive my desire to teach and learn.

This project is a reality because of the generous support provided by two very special people at Visual One Systems: David Burroughs and Eli Nadel. Through their efforts, hospitality management students will be better prepared for the challenges of a career in hotel management.

Finally, I want to thank my husband, Peter, and sons, Benjamin and Daniel. I am blessed with having them in my life.

Sheryl F. Kline, Ph.D.
Purdue University

Together we thank the reviewers of the proposal for this workbook and software package, who provided wonderful feedback. They include: Cynthia A. Angell, Cuyahoga Community College; James Bardi, Pennsylvania State University; Jill Dybus, Oakton Community College; Anne Polenchar, Hocking College; and Carl Stafford, Manchester Community College. Much thanks also is owed to our editors at John Wiley & Sons, Inc. We want to thank JoAnna Turtletaub for her friendship and support of this project. Her understanding of the hospitality education field is an invaluable and rare asset in the publishing industry today. It has been a pleasure to work with her throughout this project. We also want to thank Julie Kerr, a woman of great patience and understanding. Thank you for all the calls and e-mails and for sharing your publishing expertise. We greatly appreciate their contributions to this project.

# CHAPTER 1

# GETTING STARTED

Welcome to the demonstration system designed to help you learn the concepts of a *property management system,* or PMS as the industry refers to this technology. As you use this program, you will become skillful in the following areas of property management system technology.

- Reservations and Room Availability
- Registration
- Guest Room Posting and Check-out
- Guest Services
- Night Audit

The demonstration software is a product known as Innstar, a very successful PMS, created by. National Guest Systems. David Burroughs, who is currently the president and CEO of Visual One founded National Guest Systems in 1977. (In 1999, the name of the company was changed to Visual One.) In addition to the Innstar PMS software, Visual One offers a full line of Windows software to the hospitality industry, including Property Management, Sales & Catering, Restaurant Point-of-Sale, Back Office Accounting, and Golf Systems. The Innstar software is used by more than 1,500 hotel properties. Your software simulation package uses the Innstar software, and functions for the most part as a real hotel.

## How to Use This Demonstration Software

Innstar is loaded on both a CD and a floppy disk that will work on all Windows-based systems. The computer program resides on the CD while the data is located on the floppy disk. That means both disks must be in their respective drives every time the program is used. Also, this program is totally keyboard-driven so the mouse cannot be used with it.

To start, place the CD in the appropriate computer drive, and the 3.5 floppy in the A drive. In most systems, this will be the proper configuration. If your system has a ZIP drive, you may need to follow other directions to properly operate the software. See the directions in the systems requirements section of the workbook.

Once the disk and CD are loaded, select the "My Computer" icon on your desktop then select the drive with the Innstar CD. Open the CD and select the file Welcome.bat by locating it and selecting OK. This will start up Instar and show the menu (Figure 1.1).

Once the Welcome screen loads as shown in Figure 1.1, depress the Enter key to start the system. Pass codes are not used in this program. Therefore, every time you see a request for a pass code, use the Enter key to continue the program (Figure 1.2).

At this point you are ready to use Innstar!

```
welcome - EXEC                                                          _ □ ×
T 12 x 20 ▾
PC 1   SCREEN 01           INNSTAR  / SULLKLIN INN        09/28/00  21:44

              ┌──────────────────────────────────────┐
              │        WELCOME TO INNSTAR             │
              │                                       │
              │     ENTER PASSCODE TO CONTINUE:       │
              └──────────────────────────────────────┘

                        INNSTAR Version 17.2

                       DUAL RECORDING IS OFF

              ┌──────────────────────────────────────┐
              │  Visual One Systems                   │
              │  7361 Calhoun Place, Suite 301        │
              │  Rockville, Maryland   20855 USA      │
              │  Office: 301-926-2500                 │
              │  Fax: 301-926-0001                    │
              └──────────────────────────────────────┘

      (C)Copyright 1992-2001, Trade Secret, Visual One Systems
                     All rights reserved
                                                   0911220-000000
```

**Figure 1.1**

```
welcome - EXEC                                                          _ □ ×
T 12 x 20 ▾
PC 1   SCREEN 01           INNSTAR  / SULLKLIN INN        09/28/00  21:47

        REGISTRATION        SHIFT =           CASHIER

    ┌─────────────────────────┐      ┌─────────────────────────┐
    │ 1 = CHECK IN W/RESV     │      │ 6 = POST TO FOLIO       │
    │ 2 = WALK IN GUEST       │      │ 7 = CHECK OUT           │
    │ 3 = DISPLAY/CHANGE FOLIO│      │ 8 = RE-CHECK IN         │
    │ 4 = ROOM CHANGE         │      │ 9 = PRINT STATEMENT     │
    │ 5 = ROOM ALLOCATION     │      │ C = SHIFT REPORT        │
    │ A = ARRIVALS            │      │ P = POSTINGS SCAN       │
    └─────────────────────────┘      └─────────────────────────┘

            STATUS                            OTHER

    ┌─────────────────────────┐      ┌─────────────────────────┐
    │ B = ROOM AVAILABILITY   │      │ R = RESERVATIONS        │
    │ D = DEPARTURES          │      │ T = TELEPHONE           │
    │ K = SHOW RACK (O, V)    │      │ H = HOUSEKEEPING        │
    │ S = ROOM STATUS SCAN    │      │ M = MAINTENANCE         │
    │ X = SET ROOM STATUS     │      │ U = RESTAURANTS         │
    │ Y = SET ROOM CONDITION  │      │ F = FUNCTIONS/BANQUET   │
    │ Z = SHOW HOUSE STATUS   │      │ J = CITY LEDGER         │
    │ N = FRONT DESK REPORTS  │      │ E = TRAVEL AGENT        │
    │ Q = OTHER               │      │ G = GUEST HISTORY       │
    │ * = HELP   L = LOG OFF  │      │ W = WORD PROCESSING     │
    └─────────────────────────┘      └─────────────────────────┘
                                                   0020101-000000
```

**Figure 1.2**

## Using the Innstar Program

1. As just stated above, Innstar is a keyboard-based program and the mouse will not work with it. Innstar is driven by selecting the letter or number that is next to the function that you wish to run. For example, 1 will activate the Check-In With/reservation function.
2. The Escape (Esc) key is used to return the main system menu, you will do this often as you navigate the functions of Innstar.

## How to Exit Innstar

When you complete the tasks of the lesson that you are working on, you will need to log out of Innstar. To do this, from the main menu, select the L key and your screen will look like Figure 1.3.

At this point, type in the word "quit" and you will return to the final screen (Figure 1.4).

Now depress the Ctrl key and C key at the same time to fully exit the program and return to Windows. At this point, you can remove your CD and floppy from the PC and store them for the next lesson or assignment. Again, the CD and floppy must be in the drives to run the program every time.

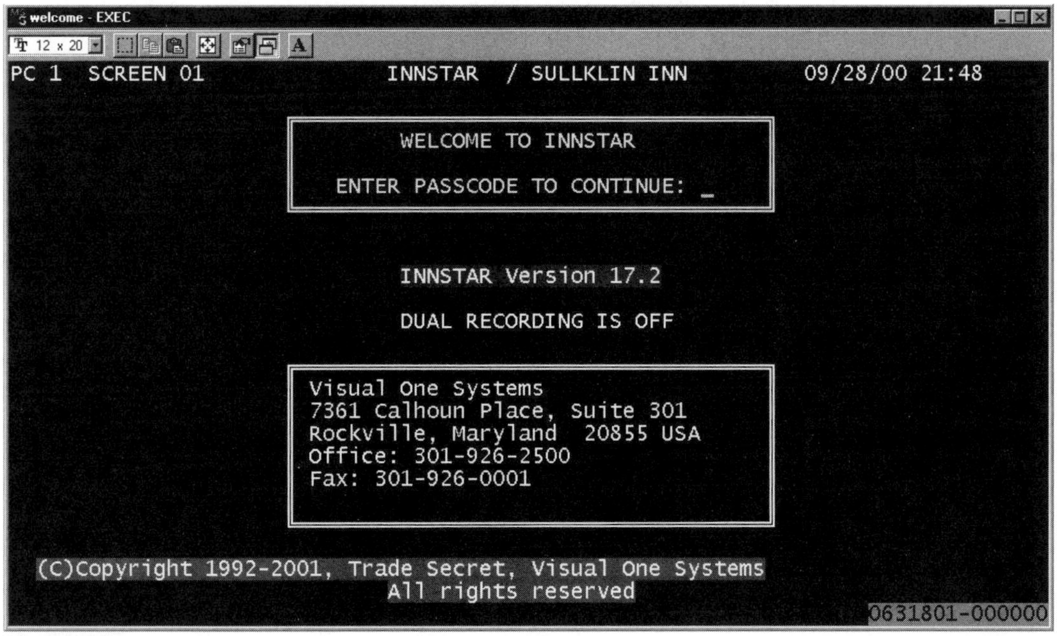

**Figure 1.3**

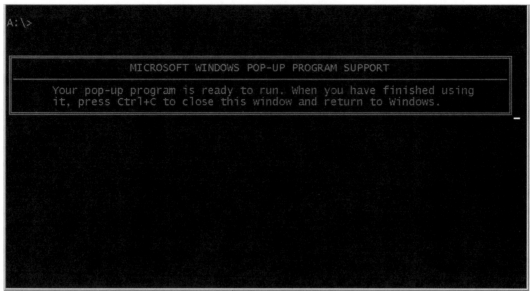

**Figure 1.4**

## Printing from Innstar

Normally, Innstar will print to the normal printer default, LPT1. In some network environments, the print command will buffer work until you log out of Innstar. As you get into some of the assignments, you will be able to test the print function and determine the configuration of your system. If you have trouble on one configuration, you may want to move your disks to a standalone PC (nonnetworked) and test the print function there.

## Clerk ID Number

All students are prompted to use an ID number when making reservations, checking-in and out guests, and doing most any function in the system. ID numbers are two-digit numbers from 01 to 12. Your ID number is based on the month you were born. For example, if you were born in January, your ID number is 01; if you were born in September, your ID number is 09. It is important to use the same ID number throughout this program.

## Description of the Hotel Property

Congratulations! You are now the proud owner of a small hotel located in Wiley, Pennsylvania, USA. This is your first day on the job, and the date is September 28, 2000. The hotel has 25 guestrooms. It has a small restaurant and two meeting rooms.

The hotel primarily serves the business traveler and small groups. It has a pool and on the weekends caters to families with children. Figure 1.5 shows the layout of the Sullklin Inn.

## Sullklin Inn

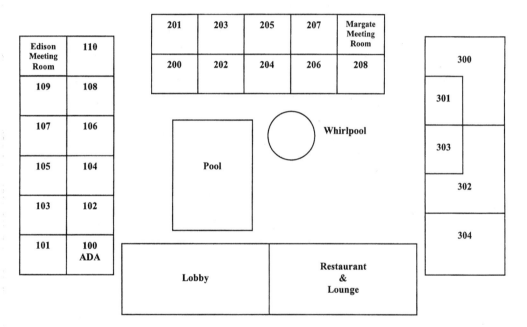

Figure 1.5

<u>**Keep This Sheet Handy for Navigating Innstar**</u>

## Summary of the Basics

<u>Pass codes</u>
There are no pass codes; just use the Enter key to bypass any pass-coded areas.

<u>Y = yes, N = no</u>
Whenever a question is asked by Innstar, respond by pressing Y for yes or N for no. Some questions default to an N or a Y so you can press the Enter key if the default is the answer you want.

<u>Cursor movements: Enter, Page Down, Down Arrow</u>
To move from field to field, use the Enter key or the PgDn (page down) and down arrow keys. The arrow keys have arrow icons on the keys.

<u>Using F-keys and the Tab key</u>
Of course, you may type out the data desired in any field. But, by using the F-keys, you will save a multitude of keystrokes. The F-keys are located at the top of the keyboard.

**Date fields:** All date fields are formatted in the month/day/year (MM/DD/YY) style used in the United States. So you may type out the date as 011500 for January 15, 2000. You may press the F1 key if you want to quickly enter today's date, the F2 key for tomorrow's date, F3 for the next day's date, and so on.

**Number fields:** In an I.D. number field, number of room field, number of night field, number of persons field, and others similar, you may use the F1 key to indicate the number 1, the F2 key for the number 2, and so on.

**Guest type, segment type, tariff type, room type, and payment method:** Not only will the F1 key automatically enter the first guest type, segment type, tariff type, room type, or payment method, but prior to entering the desired type, you may also press the Tab key. The Tab key will display a pop-up help window showing your choices of guest/segment/room/payment types and which F-key is defined to it. To enter the appropriate data from the pop-up window, you may either:

1) Press Enter to move the cursor to the desired choice, then press letter keys on the keyboard; or
2) Press Esc and then the corresponding F-key.

If you want to abort a process, use the Esc key.

To use the Interrupt function, press and hold the Ctrl key and press the X key.

Dollar-Amount Fields
In all dollar amount fields (rates, postings, deposits, etc.), you should not use the dollar sign ($) or a decimal point (.). All trailing zeros must be typed. For example: $50.00 is entered as 5000; $6.42 is entered as 642; $298.50 is entered as 29850.

Today's Date
In this PMS system, today's date is September 28, 2000.

Your ID
Remember, your ID number is based on the month that you were born. If you were born in December, your ID number is 12; if your birth month is August, your ID number is 08.

Enter your two-digit ID number here:_____.

Logging Off
From the Innstar main menu press L, then type "quit."
At the final window, hold the Ctrl key down and press C.

The Rack Rates for the room types are:

| Double Double | DD | $  85.00 |
| King | K | $ 100.00 |
| Suite | SUIT | $ |

## System Requirements

To operate the demonstration version of the Innstar Property Management software that accompanies this text, you will need the following computer hardware.

- IBM-compatible processor — Pentium or above. (The software does not support Macintosh technology.)
- Microsoft Windows 95 operating system or above.
- A PC with a connected diskette drive for 1.44 Mb floppy and a CD drive. The software requires that both be operational to run the program.

Note the following regarding operation: The program does not copy any files to the hard drive or any networked drive. And if there are other disk drives, such as a ZIP drive, you must insert a blank disk, or the program may not operate properly. Finally, the PC must be connected to a local or network printer for the various exercises the text will instruct you to run.

## Chapter 1 Exercises

Name _____ Date _____

1) Load the Innstar program by following the directions in this chapter. When you get to the main screen, look at the top part of the screen to answer this question.
   a)  What is the name of the hotel?_____

   b)  What date appears on the top right of Innstar's main menu? _____

2) This hotel and Wiley, Pennsylvania, are virtual, not real places. Using your imagination, describe the property and the city in which it is located. Make this property as real as possible, give it a brief history and present-day. What are the target markets? What type of business does it attract? What does it look like and how is it designed?

   _____

   _____

   _____

   _____

   _____

   _____

   _____

   _____

   _____

3) What keys are used to move the cursor in this program?

   _____

4) How is the computer's mouse used in this program?

   _____

5) Describe where the F-keys are located on your computer equipment.

   _____

# CHAPTER 2

# RESERVATIONS

## Key Learning Concepts in Chapter 2
- How to create a reservation.
- Steps in the reservation process.
- How to retrieve and display a reservation.
- How to cancel and reactivate a reservation.
- How to make a group block and book a room from a group block.
- How to describe and analyze the information contained in the room availability, daily summary, and daily booking screens.
- How to handle special reservations issues, including share-with and advance deposit functions.

## The Reservation Process

The reservation process begins when the guest contacts the property to reserve a room. This can be done in a variety of ways. Guests contact the hotel via telephone, Internet, fax, mail, and the hotel brand's central reservation system. For the purpose of this workbook, all reservations will be made via the telephone.

The reservation process involves more than just taking an order to reserve a hotel room. It is an opportunity to make a good first impression. The hotel reservationist represents the hotel to the guest. A reservationist's attitude, professionalism, and ability to take a reservation efficiently and accurately are critical to establishing a good first impression of the property.

## Reservation Process in Innstar

To enter the reservation area of the Innstar program, press the R key for the main reservation screen (Figure 2.1).

The primary Reservations screen contains the functions for the reservation process. There are three areas on the reservation screen, including two boxes on the left side of the screen. The top box, labeled GUESTS, contains the functions involved in the guest reservation process. The GUESTS area is used to create, change, display, and cancel a reservation for an individual guest or guests that are not part of a group. The bottom box, labeled GROUPS, contains all the group reservation functions. The large area on the right side of the screen is used to display screens that provide summary information about availability and status information. This information is helpful to reservationists and room reservation managers.

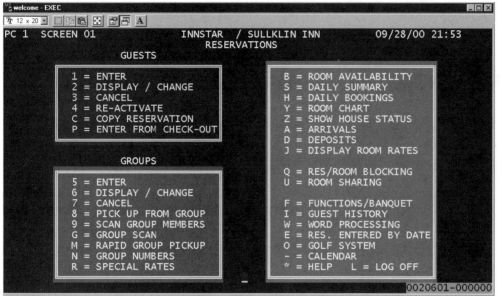

**Figure 2.1**

## How to Make a Basic Reservation

In this case, a guest calls the property and would like to reserve one room for two adults and one child. They plan to arrive on April 21, 2001, and stay for two nights. Enter the reservation screen R and press 1 to ENTER an individual reservation.

The fields on this screen (Figure 2.2) and succeeding reservation screens will guide the reservationist through the basic reservation process. To begin taking a reservation, enter the date the guest plans to arrive. The date is entered numerically in this sequence: month, day, and year. For example April 21, 2001, is entered: "04 21 01."

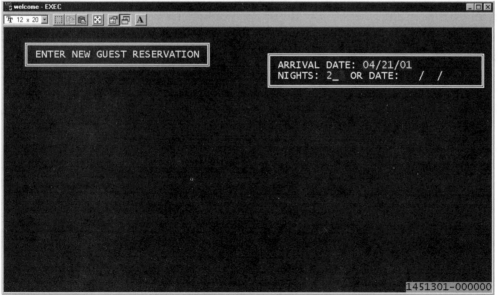

**Figure 2.2**

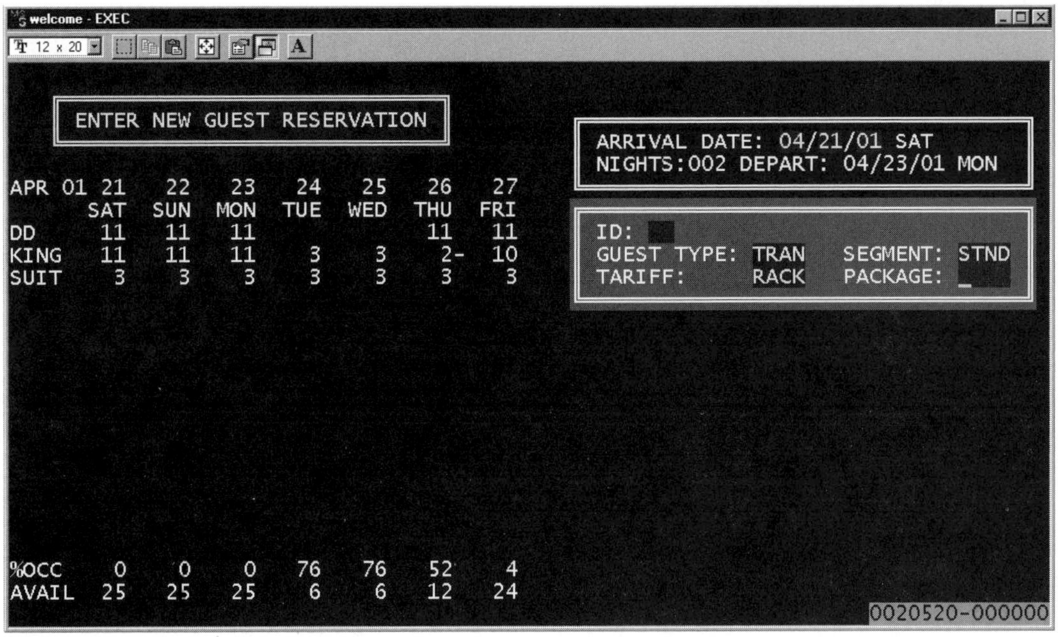

**Figure 2.3**

Next enter either the number of nights the guest plans to stay or the date the guest plans to leave the hotel. The field for a number of nights is a three-digit field. For two nights, enter "2" or "002."

Once the information is completed, the program moves to the ENTER NEW GUEST RESERVATION screen (Figure 2.3).

GUEST: This data field applies to the type of guest.
　　TRAN: Transient guests are those who call the property to make a reservation and are not affiliated with any group or special category of guest type.
　　CORP: Corporate guests receive a corporate rate, which is usually a discounted rate offered to business travelers.
　　WALK: A guest who arrives at the hotel without a room reservation and requests an accommodation. This person is called a "walk-in." Front-desk agents usually check in a walk-in via the Registration functions on the main screen. However, some hotels create a reservation first and then register the walk-in.
　　GOV: This type of guest is traveling on government business and is usually given a special discounted government rate.
SEGMENT: This field identifies each guest by his or her target market segment. Most guests will belong to the standard target market.
　　STND: This segment is for the regular guest. The majority of guests who place reservations are standard guests.
　　SPEC: Special guests are identified as belonging to a special target market. For example, corporate, government, and group bookings would be identified as special guests.
TARIFF: There are only two choices for this field. This field identifies the guest based on the room rate that he or she receives.

RACK:  These guests will be paying the rack rate, or the highest standard rate that the hotel charges per night.

SPEC:  These guests receive a discounted rate for the room. Usually corporate and government employees traveling on business receive a discounted rate. Groups also receive rates that are discounted from the rack rate.

PACKAGE:  This field is used to identify any package plans that the hotel offers. A package could include a room rate, meals, and/or tickets for an event. This property does not offer packages, so use the F1 or Enter key to skip this field.

Enter your two-digit ID number. Then complete the GUEST, SEGMENT, TARIFF, and PACKAGE information. Figure 2.3 displays an example of the pop-up help menu for the GUEST TYPE field. All of these fields, except the PACKAGE field, have a preidentified list of options that have been created by management. Either type the information or use the corresponding F-keys to complete each field.

For the first  Reservation example, 1, enter the following information: This guest is a transient, so enter F1 (see Figure 2.4). This guest is a standard guest who is receiving the rack rate, so press F1 in both the SEGMENT and TARIFF fields. To skip the PACKAGE field, press the Enter key. This program offers pop-up help menus for each of these fields. To view the options for a field, move the cursor to the field and press the Tab key. The pop-up help field will display the options. Press the Esc key to return to the field and use the F-keys or type in the information.

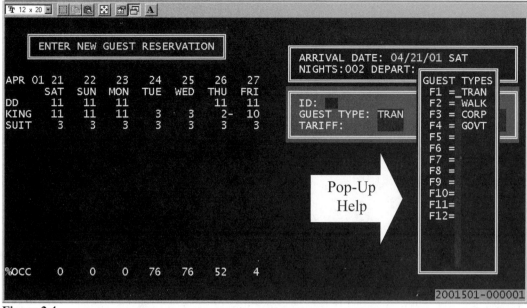

**Figure 2.4**

---

### How to Read the Table in Figure 2.4

Each field is used to reserve different room types for the reservation. Most reservations require one room and one room type, therefore only the first field is completed. If a guest requests two different room types, then two fields would be completed. For example, two fields are completed when a guest requests one double-bedded room and one king-bedded room.

Look at the table on the left side of the screen to determine the desired room type. The left column of the table shows the room type. This hotel has double-bedded rooms, rooms with two double beds, king-bedded rooms, rooms with one king bed, and suites. The days and dates are displayed at the top of this table, beginning with the arrival date. Notice that this hotel has three room types displayed as DD, KING, and "SUIT."

The numbers within this table represent the number of rooms that are available to sell by room type for each night. A minus sign (–) represents the number of rooms oversold. A blank space denotes the facts that no rooms are available. In the example, there are 11 double-bedded rooms available on April 23, and no double-bedded rooms available on April 24 and 25. On April 26, the king-bedded rooms are oversold by two rooms.

---

Complete this information by filling in the ADULT/CHILD, ROOM TYPE, # OF ROOMS, and RATES fields (Figure 2.5), as defined below. This reservation is for two adults and one child. They requested one room with two double beds (DD).

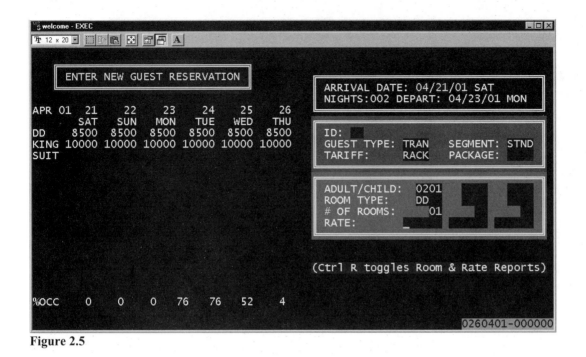

**Figure 2.5**

ADULT/CHILD:  To enter the number of adults, type the number using one or two digits. For example, two adults are entered as "02." To enter adults and children, use four digits. Two adults and one child are entered as "0201."

ROOM TYPE:  Select the room type either by using the F-keys or by typing in the room type. A room with two double beds is a DD, a room with a king bed is a KING.  Either type "DD" or press the F1 key.

# OF ROOMS: Use two digits to enter the number of rooms.  One room would be entered "01." F-keys may also be used: F1 equals 1 room, F2 equals two rooms, and so on.  Use the FI key to request one room.

RATE: Management sets the rack and special rates. Press the Ctrl key and the R key on the keyboard to display the rates for each reservation. Rates are entered by using only numbers. Do not use the dollar sign or decimal points when entering rates.  For example, $100.00 is entered 10000.  The rate for this reservation is $85.00. Enter this rate by typing "8500."

After the rate is entered the curser moves to the next red field on the screen.  There are two such fields.  Skip the two red fields by using  the Page Down key to move to the next step in the reservation process. After the rate information has been entered, the next screen displays the total room, total tax, and total room and tax amount (Figure 2.6).  The reservationist may or may not share this information with the guest at this time.  To move to the next screen, press the Enter key.

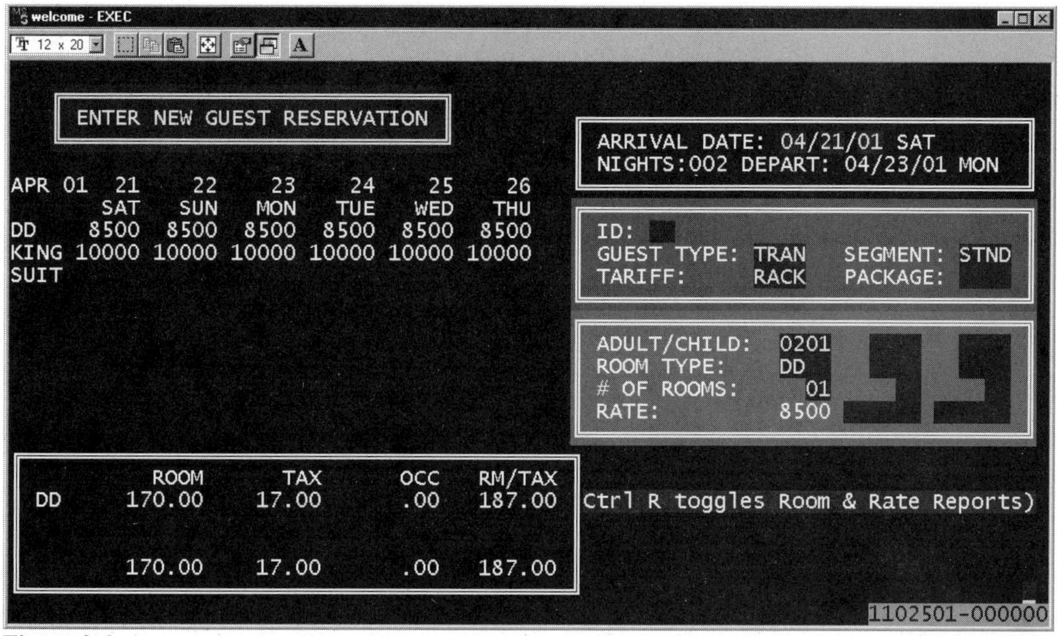

**Figure 2.6**

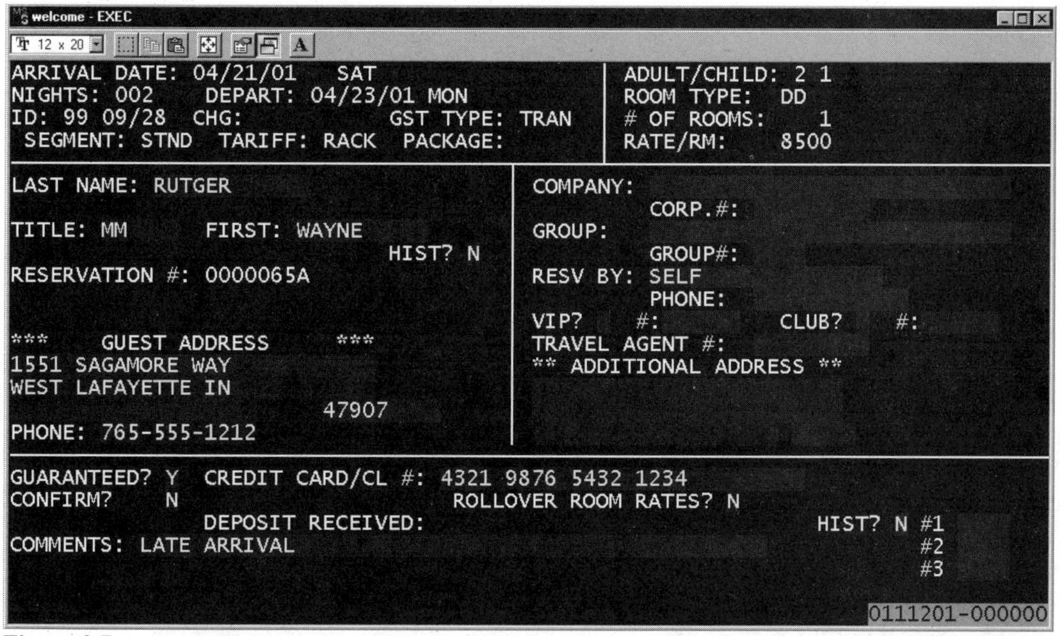

**Figure 2.7**

Figure 2.7 displays the fields where the basic reservation data are entered. Accuracy is extremely important throughout the reservation process, in particular for the guest name fields. Misspelled last names and incorrect arrival dates create problems in both the reservation and registration processes. For example, it is difficult to locate a reservation when a guest's last name has been misspelled or when the arrival date has been incorrectly entered. Reservation information is also used during the registration process. An accurate and complete reservation record speeds up the check-in process and ensures a good customer service experience.

Name fields: Enter the guest's last name, title, and first name. Press the Enter key after each entry to fill up the data field.

HIST:  HIST is short for guest history. Some hotels use this information for guest service and marketing purposes. The hotel may track details concerning the guest's frequency of visits, corporate affiliation, zip code, or special requests. This hotel does not use guest history, so enter N for no, to continue.

RESERVATION #:  This number is generated automatically by the computer. It is used to locate reservations in the system. The reservationist will tell the guest this number, who can use it to confirm the creation of this reservation record.  Because each system generates a reservation number, your number may be different than the one shown in the workbook.

GUEST ADDRESS: Use this field to enter the guest's mailing address, city, state, zip or postal code, and country information.

PHONE: Enter the phone information, area code first.  Numbers and dashes (-) may be used in this field.

Now enter the guest information. The reservation is for Mr. and Mrs. Wayne Rutger, who live at 1551 Sagamore Way in West Lafayette, Indiana, 47907. The reservation is guaranteed with a credit card.  Enter the card number as "4321 9876 5432 1234." The family plans to arrive very late in the evening. Enter the note "LATE ARRIVAL" on the comment line of the screen. Your screen should look like the example given in the workbook (Figure 2.7).  If your screen does not look like the example, or if you made a mistake, continue on with the reservation. You will have an opportunity to go back and make changes and correct the information.

Use the Enter key to move to the next screen (Figure 2.8). This screen includes a pop-up menu. If you would like to make any changes to the ACCOMMODATIONS area, press 1. If you want to make changes to the BASIC DATA area, press 2. The ACCOMMODATIONS portion is located at the top of the screen and includes the arrival and departure date information. The BASIC DATA area includes the guest name and address.

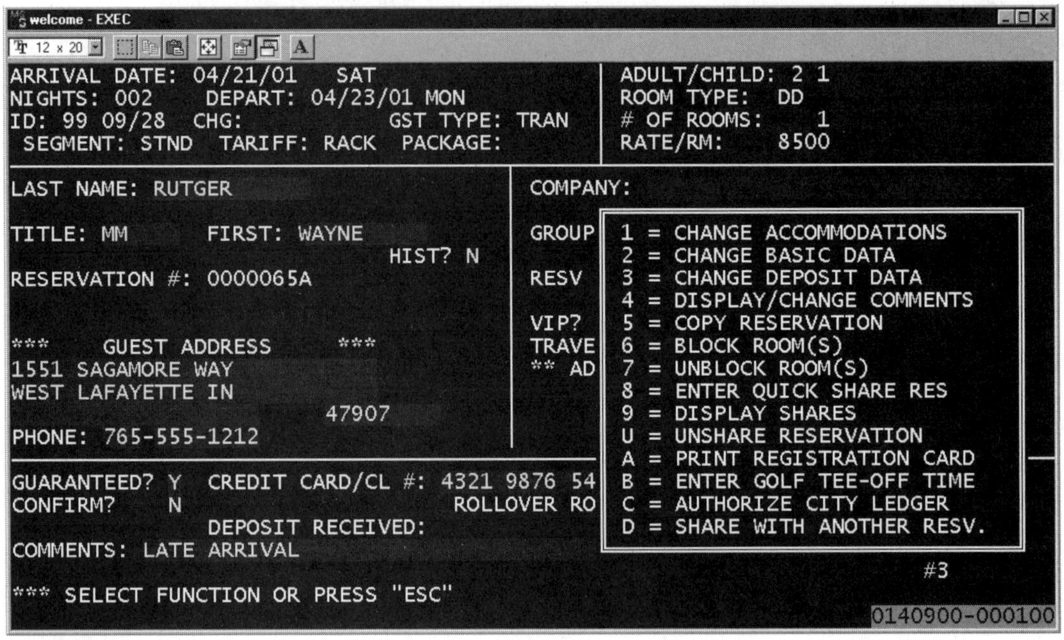

**Figure 2.8**

If you are satisfied with the reservation, use the Esc key to return to the main menu. Congratulations! You have successfully completed your first reservation!

## How to Retrieve and Display a Reservation

After a reservation record has been created, it is stored in the reservation part of the system. There are many reasons why a reservationist would revisit an existing reservation record. At this time, he or she might check for accuracy and correct errors on existing reservations. Also guests call the property to change their reservations. Some common examples include guests who want to change arrival or departure dates, guarantee, or even cancel the reservation.

For example, you receive a call from Louis Good. He has a guaranteed reservation for November 20, 2001, and wishes to change his arrival date to November 21, 2001. Enter the reservation screen from the main menu by pressing the R key and then the 2 key (Figure 2.9). Now type the first four letters of the guest's last name, in this case, "GOOD," then press the Page Down key.

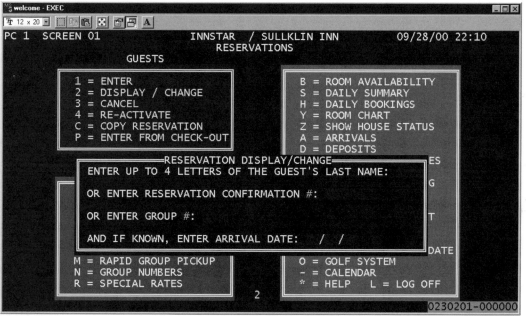

**Figure 2.9**

```
welcome - EXEC                                                        _ □ ✕
T 12 x 20    ▣ ▣ ▣ ▣  ▣ ▣ A
ARRIVAL DATE: 11/21/00  TUE          ADULT/CHILD: 1
NIGHTS: 001  DEPARTING: 11/22/00  WED   ROOM TYPE:  KING
ID: 04 09/27  CHG: 99 09/27  GST TYPE: CORP  # OF ROOMS:    1
 SEGMENT: SPEC  TARIFF: SPEC  PACKAGE:    RATE/RM:   9000

LAST NAME: GOOD                      COMPANY: OUTLET MALL MANAGEMENT

TITLE: MR      FIRST: LOUIS         GROUP  ┌──────────────────────────────┐
                                           │ 1 = CHANGE ACCOMMODATIONS    │
RESERVATION #: 00000649             RESV   │ 2 = CHANGE BASIC DATA        │
                                           │ 3 = CHANGE DEPOSIT DATA      │
                                    VIP?   │ 4 = DISPLAY/CHANGE COMMENTS  │
***     GUEST ADDRESS     ***       TRAVE  │ 5 = COPY RESERVATION         │
353 WYOMISSING BLVD                 ** AD  │ 6 = BLOCK ROOM(S)            │
READING, PA                                │ 7 = UNBLOCK ROOM(S)          │
                   19604                   │ 8 = ENTER QUICK SHARE RES    │
PHONE: 610-555-5353                        │ 9 = DISPLAY SHARES           │
                                           │ U = UNSHARE RESERVATION      │
                                           │ A = PRINT REGISTRATION CARD  │
GUARANTEED? Y  CREDIT CARD/CL #: 3003 4004 50 B = ENTER GOLF TEE-OFF TIME │
CONFIRM?   N                   ROLLOVER RO  │ C = AUTHORIZE CITY LEDGER    │
          DEPOSIT RECEIVED:                │ D = SHARE WITH ANOTHER RESV. │
COMMENTS: CORP DISCOUNT                     └──────────────────────────────┘
ENTER MODIFIER ID#:                                        #3 0000
*** SELECT FUNCTION OR PRESS "ESC"
                                                  0231401-000000
```

**Figure 2.10**

When the reservation appears, enter Y for yes and display this reservation. After you type "Y," a pop-up menu appears on the right side of the screen (Figure 2.10). Most changes are made in the ACCOMMODATIONS or BASIC DATA areas. The ACCOMMODATIONS area is where you'll make changes in arrival and departure dates, as well as room type, number of rooms, number of guests, and rate information. BASIC DATA is where you'll enter changes to the guest's name, address, and other demographic information.

In this case, the guest would like to change his arrival date, so enter "1" to change the accommodation data.

Before making any change of arrival or departure dates, check the availability chart to ensure that you have rooms available to accommodate the guest's request. Enter the date change by typing "11 21 01." Now use the Page Down key to move through the remaining fields. At the bottom of the reservation, enter your ID number in the appropriate field.

If you are satisfied with the changes, press the Esc key; if not, go back using the pop-up help menu to guide you.

Congratulations! You have successfully changed the arrival date for this reservation.

## How to Cancel a Reservation

Reservations that have been created may be cancelled at any time. When guests contact the hotel to cancel a reservation, they are releasing a previously reserved room. This helps the management maintain accurate records and plan for future business.

It is important to cancel the correct reservation record to avoid unnecessary problems in the future. The reservationist should double-check the guest's name and address prior to canceling a reservation. Once the correct reservation is identified, the cancellation process may begin. The reservationist records the reason for cancellation along with the name of the person who is canceling the reservation. Quite often, a person other than the guest is canceling the reservation. This is especially true for corporate guests.

For example, Mr. Lee Anulara has changed his plans and needs to cancel his reservation. His reservation is for September 28, 2000. To cancel a reservation, enter the reservation screen by pressing R and then 3 (Figure 2.11). At this screen, type the first four letters of the guest's last name, in this case, "ANUL," and his arrival date, in this case, "09 28 00."

Once the reservation record appears, double-check to make sure it is the right reservation record. Ask the caller for the name, address, and phone number for this reservation. If he or she gives the correct information, go ahead and cancel the reservation. In this example, the caller states that the reservation is for Mr. Lee Anulara at 1776 Rios Road in San Diego, California. Select Y to cancel this reservation.

After you enter "Y," a box opens. At this point, you ask the caller for his or her name and for the reason that he or she is canceling the reservation. Our caller is the guest himself. So type "SELF" and then your ID code. The reason for canceling is that the guest is not coming, so enter "01."

Before ending the conversation, it is important to thank the guest for canceling the reservation and to tell him the cancellation number. Note that the computer program assigns the cancellation number so your cancellation number may be different from that in the example. The cancellation number given in this workbook, 30928, is shown in Figure 2.12.

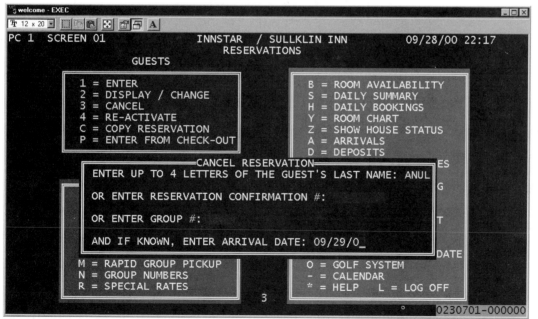

**Figure 2.11**

To end the cancellation process and return to the main menu, press Esc. Before ending the call, ask the guest if he would like to reserve a room for another visit. A cancellation is an opportunity to book future business! In this case, the guest does not want to book another reservation at this time.

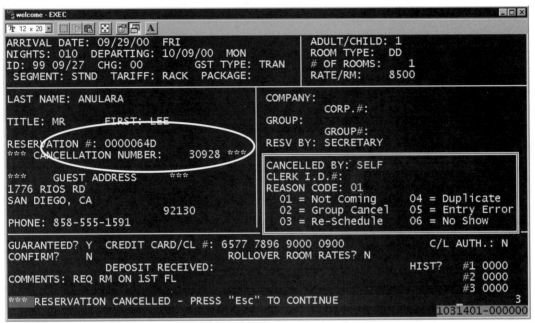

```
 welcome - EXEC                                                    _ □ ×
 T 12 x 20 ▾  □ ⌹ ⌹ ⊠ ⌹ ⌹ A
ARRIVAL DATE: 09/29/00  FRI           ADULT/CHILD: 1
NIGHTS: 010  DEPARTING: 10/09/00 MON  ROOM TYPE:  DD
ID: 99 09/27  CHG: 00        GST TYPE: TRAN  # OF ROOMS:   1
 SEGMENT: STND  TARIFF: RACK  PACKAGE:       RATE/RM:   8500

LAST NAME: ANULARA                    COMPANY:
                                              CORP.#:
TITLE: MR      FIRST: LEE             GROUP:
                                              GROUP#:
RESERVATION #: 0000064D               RESV BY: SECRETARY
*** CANCELLATION NUMBER:    30928 ***
                                      ┌─────────────────────────────────┐
***     GUEST ADDRESS      ***        │CANCELLED BY: SELF               │
1776 RIOS RD                          │CLERK I.D.#:                     │
SAN DIEGO, CA                         │REASON CODE: 01                  │
                   92130              │  01 = Not Coming  04 = Duplicate │
PHONE: 858-555-1591                   │  02 = Group Cancel 05 = Entry Error│
                                      │  03 = Re-Schedule 06 = No Show   │
                                      └─────────────────────────────────┘
GUARANTEED? Y  CREDIT CARD/CL #: 6577 7896 9000 0900     C/L AUTH.: N
CONFIRM?   N                    ROLLOVER ROOM RATES? N
           DEPOSIT RECEIVED:                         HIST?  #1 0000
COMMENTS: REQ RM ON 1ST FL                                  #2 0000
                                                            #3 0000
*** RESERVATION CANCELLED - PRESS "Esc" TO CONTINUE               3
                                                     1031401-000000
```

**Figure 2.12**

## How to Reactivate a Reservation

There are several reasons why a cancelled reservation may be reactivated and placed back into the active reservation status. The guest may change his or her mind; or perhaps the wrong reservation was cancelled and needs to be reinstated. All cancelled reservations are removed from the hotel's reservation system and are not part of the hotel's future availability. They do, however, remain in the system and may be viewed by going into the RESERVATIONS, R, area and pressing the 4 key (Figure 2.13).

For example, Dr. Sourav Shah had a reservation for October 14, 2000, but cancelled it. His plans have changed again and he is contacting the hotel to re-reserve a room for the same date.

To locate his cancelled reservation, go to the reservation screen by pressing the R and 4 keys (Figure 2.14) to reactivate his original reservation. Enter the first four letters of his last name, "SHAH," and press the Enter key until you reach the arrival date field; there, enter "10 10 01."

The screen should look like the one in your workbook. If it does, enter Y for yes and R to reactivate it. Press Esc and return to the main menu.

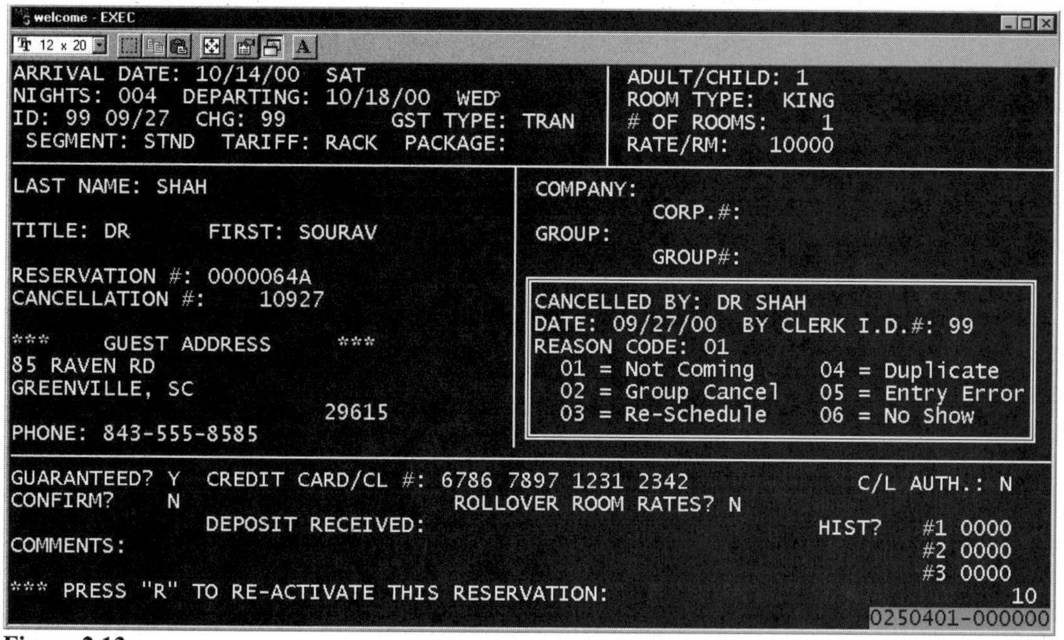

Figure 2.13

Figure 2.14

## How to Make a Group Block

Groups comprise more than one room, often of 10 rooms or more. A representative from the group or professional travel planner contacts the hotel to reserve a set of rooms. This is usually handled by the hotel's sales department or by a designated member of the reservation team who specializes in handling groups.

There are many different types of groups. Groups can be part of a larger citywide convention or set up for family functions such as weddings. Some types of groups include corporate meetings, church retreats, school teams, and vacation tour groups.

A two-step method is used to handle groups: blocking and then booking rooms. When groups reserve rooms at a hotel, the hotel sets up a room block to hold a set number of rooms during the period of time designated by the group making the reservation. Blocking and booking rooms are two different concepts. A room is considered booked when a name is assigned to a room. This can be done via a rooming list that contains the list of names in the group, or each individual may contact the hotel separately. When rooms are booked on an individual basis, each person contacts the hotel and makes a reservation from the room block. When this occurs, it is called a "pick up" from the room block. The next case involves creating a room block.

For example, a prominent local family has chosen your property to hold their tenth annual family reunion.  The Josiah Smith family would like to reserve 10 rooms beginning on December 16, 2000, for two nights.  To access the group reservation area of the program, press R for RESERVATIONS and 5 to set up the group block.  The group number for this group is determined by management and is group number 1011. Enter the group number, "1011," your ID, and the arrival date, "12 16 00" (Figure 2.15). Since this is a family function and most of the relatives have children, this group would like to book rooms with two double beds. Check the availability table on the left side of the screen.   There are 11 double-bedded rooms available on December 16 and 17, therefore the hotel can accommodate this group's request.

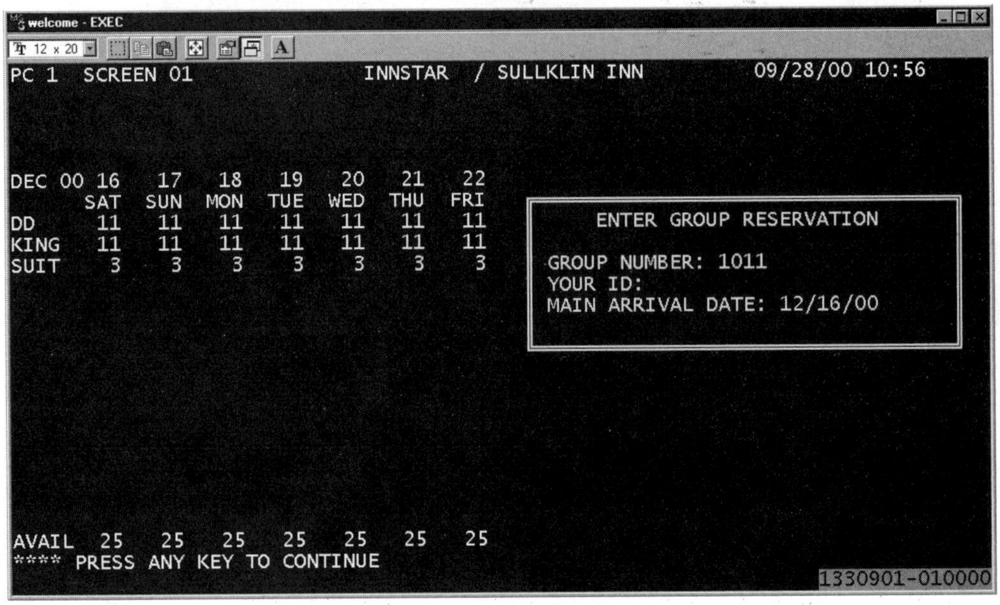

**Figure 2.15**

Complete the data fields and hit the Enter key to move to the next screen. Now enter the arrival date of December 16, 2000, as "12 16 00."

The release date refers to the date when the rooms on the block that have not been used are released into the hotel's room-availability inventory. For example, let's say that by December 10, the Smith group booked only eight rooms from the block. After the release date, the group would not hold any rooms. The remaining two rooms would be released and made available to any guest who requests them. The release date for this group is December 10, 2000. Enter this date by typing "12 10 00." The GUEST TYPE is transient and the SEGMENT is standard. Press the F1 key for those fields. The group is receiving a special discounted rate for two reasons: first, because they are reserving 10 rooms and, second, because that weekend is a low-demand period, therefore the rates are heavily discounted. Use the F2 key to view the special rate in the TARIFF field. Skip the PACKAGE field by pressing the Enter key.

The name of the group is the "Smith Family Reunion" and the address is in care of Tonya Smith at her home address. Enter the information as shown in Figure 2.16. Skip the HIST ACC# and the IATA# fields by pressing Enter twice. Ms. Tonya Smith is going to pay for all the rooms and tax, but each individual is responsible for any other charges, such as food or telephone charges. To reflect this, enter "BILL ROOM AND TAX ONLY" in the comment line. To complete this screen, hit the Enter key and move to the next screen to enter the group reservation information.

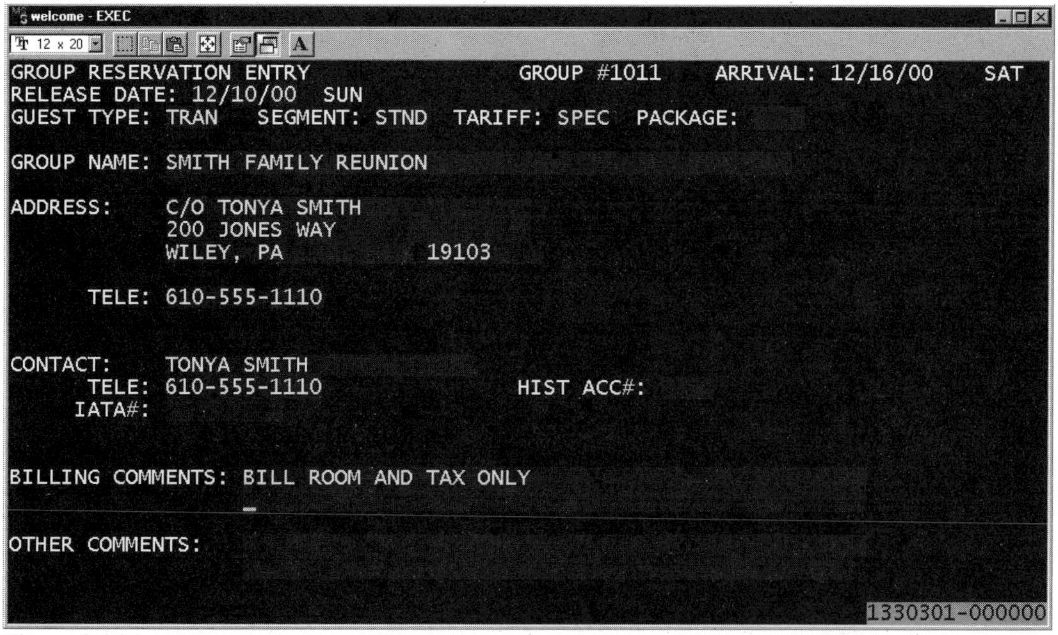

Figure 2.16

To complete this group booking, enter the following information (Figure 2.17). The group will arrive on December 16, 2000, and stay two nights. They are requesting 10 double double-bedded rooms. They will receive a very special discounted rate of $60.00 per night. Enter the date by typing "12 16 00" and the number of nights as "2." To enter the ROOM TYPE, either use the F1 key or type "DD." Type the number "10" and then "4," respectively, for the NUMBER OF ROOMS and NUMBER OF GUESTS in a room. Now enter the rate; do not use a decimal point; type only the numbers: "6000." Hit the Enter key and answer N for no. There is no need to block any more rooms at this time, because this group only requested double double-bedded rooms arriving on the same date.

Congratulations. You have just booked your first group reservation! You are now ready to pick up a room from a room block.

## How to Book a Room from a Room Block

You use the PICK UP FROM ROOMS group function when an individual who is part of a group contacts the hotel to make a reservation. To enter the group pick-up area, press R for RESERVATIONS and 8 for PICK UP FROM ROOMS.

You may have noticed that when you press R for RESERVATIONS there is another group pick-up function called RAPID GROUP PICK UP; it is accessed by pressing M. This is used when the hotel receives a rooming list. The next case involves an individual who is calling to place an individual reservation, not from a rooming list.

```
welcome - EXEC                                                        _ □ ×
 T 12 x 20                     A
                        ENTER GROUP RESERVATION
                           GROUP NUMBER: 1011
GROUP NAME: SMITH FAMILY REUNION


DEC 00 16    17    18    19    20    21    22
       SAT   SUN   MON   TUE   WED   THU   FRI
DD      1     1    11    11    11    11    11          ARRIVAL: 12/16/00
KING   11    11    11    11    11    11    11
SUIT    3     3     3     3     3     3     3          NIGHTS: 2

                                                      ROOM TYPE: DD

                                                      NUMBER OF ROOMS: 10

                                                      NUMBER OF GUESTS: 4

                                                      RATE:    6000




AVAIL  15    15    25    25    25    25    25
**** ENTER MORE ROOMS? _ (Y OR N)
                                              1332001-010000
```

**Figure 2.17**

For example, Lucinda Hampton works for Daniels Energy Company and will be attending a meeting being held at your property.  She plans to arrive on October 3 and stay for three nights. To book her reservation from the group block, press R for RESERVATIONS and 8 to pick up a group room. The name of the group is Daniels Energy Group; its group number is 1010. Type the first four letters of the group name, "DANI," and or the group number, "1010," to find this group block (Figure 2.18). Hit the Enter key to move to the next screen. It is also possible to locate the group block using one piece of information. For example, most guests know only the name of the group. It is possible to retrieve the group block using the name only, thereby skipping the other fields, by hitting the Enter or Page Down key.

Enter the information for Lucinda Hampton's reservation (Figure 2.19). Enter "1" in the ACCOMMODATIONS FIELD. It lists the accommodation type that has been blocked. This group has only one type of accommodation. Note also that at the time of this booking there were 10 rooms on the block and 9 rooms left. Enter the guest's name, address, and phone information, as shown in the workbook.  This hotel does not use guest history so answer N in the HIST field. The guest made this reservation herself so enter "SELF" in the RESV BY field and skip the PHONE field.  This reservation is guaranteed with a credit card.  Select Y in the GUARANTEED FIELD and enter the credit card number as shown in the example.

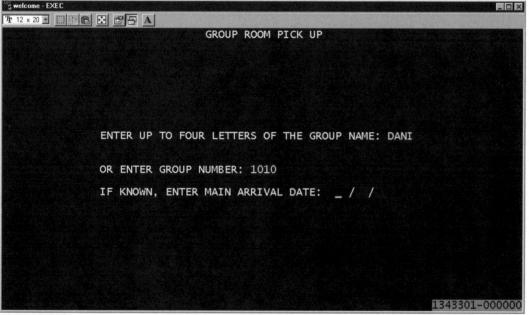

**Figure 2.18**

```
welcome - EXEC                                                          _ □ ☒
 T  12 x 20 ▾  ▢ ▢ ▢  ☒ ☒  ▢ ▢  A
PICK UP ROOM FROM   GROUP # 1010 DANIELS ENERGY GROUP
YOUR I.D.: 99                 LINE  DATE    NITES TYPE TOT  LEFT GST  RATE
ACCOMMODATIONS LINE:1    ROOMS: 1   1. 10/03/00   3 KING  10   9   1  70.00

LAST:  HAMPTON
TITLE: MS        FIRST: LUCINDA
                  HIST: N
1230 MERCURY LANE
ATLANTA, GA
                 30080

TEL: 770-5551230    PACKAGE:
COMPANY: DANIELS ENERGY

RESV BY: SELF
   PHONE:
                        IATA#:

GUARANTEED? Y     CR CARD / CL#: 3708 8889 4560 1234        C/L AUTH.: N
CONFIRM?    N     VIP? N #:       CLUB? N  #:


*** RESERVATION # 0000065C COMPLETED
MODIFY THIS RESERVATION?
                                              0140914-000100
```

**Figure 2.19**

Answer no by selecting N in the CONFIRM, VIP, and CLUB fields, and use the Enter key in the #: fields. When you are done, you may make changes to this reservation by entering Y; if you are satisfied with it, enter N for no. Now use the Esc key to return to the main menu.

## Analyzing Reservation Status Screens

Management uses several status screens to track the hotel's future room availability and reservation status information. There are a many reservation reports and information available through this program. To see a list, enter R for RESERVATIONS; the reservation information screens are located on the right side of the screen in the green box. For the purposes of this exercise, we will focus on four status reports.

The first screen is one that a reservation manager uses very frequently: the ROOM AVAILABILITY chart. There are several ways to locate the ROOM AVAILABILITY chart. Either press B on the main menu or, if you are in the RESERVATIONS menu, press R. The B key will also bring up the ROOM AVAILIBILITY screen. Once at the screen, the system prompts you to enter a date. Either type the date by using the standard format for this system or use the F1 key for today's date (September 28, 2000), F2 for tomorrow's date, and F3 for the day after tomorrow.

For example, to view the ROOM AVAILIBILITY screen from the main menu, enter B. Enter today's date by pressing the F1 key. The example in the workbook may look different fro, what you are viewing on the screen; however, by understanding the example given here, you will be able to interpret the ROOM AVAILABILITY chart in your hotel.

Along the top of the screen (Figure 2.20) are the dates for 14 days beginning with the date you entered, in this case, September 28, 2000. On the left side is a vertical list of room types. At the bottom next to the word BEDDED is the summary of all the rooms that are available on a given date. The numbers located in the middle of this chart show the number of rooms available by room type for each of the dates displayed. Take note of the column of numbers within the rectangle in the middle of the example. This column shows the availability for Wednesday, October 4, 2000. It shows the double-double rooms (DD) are over sold by one room. The blank space indicates that the king-bedded rooms are sold out. There is three suites (SUIT) available on that date.

The bottom of the column shows a summary of the availability status for that date. There are two rooms in the BEDDED area; this means that there is a total of two rooms available to sell on October 4. This number is calculated by adding-1 DD, plus 0 KING, plus 3 SUIT. Although the hotel is oversold in one room type, there are still two rooms available to sell for that evening.

The last number in the column is the occupancy percentage. On Wednesday, October 4, the hotel has a 92% occupancy percentage. The formula for calculating occupancy percentage is:

$$\text{Total rooms sold} / \text{Total rooms available} \times 100 = \text{Occupancy Percentage}$$
$$23 / 25 \times 100 = 92\% \text{ occupancy on October 4, 2000}$$

```
welcome - EXEC                                                    _ □ ×
 T 12 x 20 ▾  □ ▯ ▤  ▤  ▤ ▤  A
ROOM AVAILABILITY BY ROOM TYPE        09/28/00   11:33
SEP 00     28   29   30   01   02   03   04   05   06   07   08   09   10   11
           THU  FRI  SAT  SUN  MON  TUE  WED  THU  FRI  SAT  SUN  MON  TUE  WED

    DD      8    9   10   10   10        1-   1-   11   11   11   11   11   11
    KING    5    8   10   10   10              1   11   11   11   11   11   11
    SUIT    3    3    3    3    3    3    3    3    3    3    3    3    3    3

 BEDDED    16   20   23   23   23    3    2    3   25   25   25   25   25   25
 % OCC.    36   20    8    8    8   88   92   88    0    0    0    0    0    0
```

```
     PG/DOWN = NEXT, PG/UP = LAST, "S" = SUMMARY ,"D" = DAILY, PRINTER#:
                                                         0321301-000000
```

**Figure 2.20**

A manager would use this screen to determine rates and to decide whether to sell or not sell rooms due to availability. For example, on a date when many rooms are available, a manager might open lower rates and offer discounted rates in the hopes of increasing room sales. On days when the hotel has high occupancy, special rates would not be offered; only rack rates would be made available. When the hotel is sold out, managers may choose to stop selling rooms and close dates by not allowing any more reservations.

For example, another screen used by managers is the DAILY SUMMARY REPORT. Press the R key for RESERVATIONS and the S key to view the DAILY SUMMARY REPORT. There are three ways to view this information (Figure 2.21).

Let's look at option number 1 to SHOW TOTALS FOR TWO WEEK PERIOD. Press 1 and then the F1 for today's date.

The top of Figure 2.22 shows the dates starting with September 28 for a two-week period. Within the table the number of rooms that are check-ins, stay-overs, and check-outs are listed for each arrival date. Below the dotted line the number of rooms available for each date is displayed. Below that line is the number of rooms sold. Press the Esc key and return to the main menu.

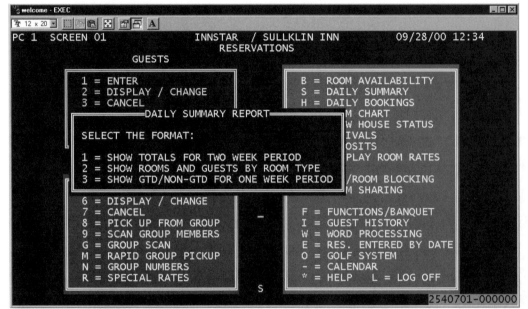

**Figure 2.21**

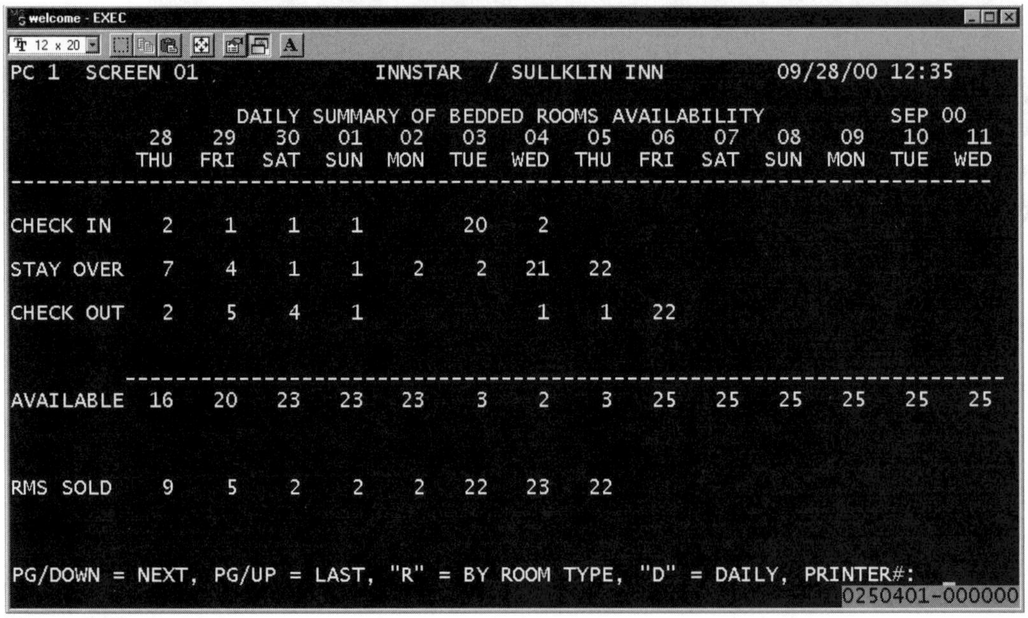

**Figure 2.22**

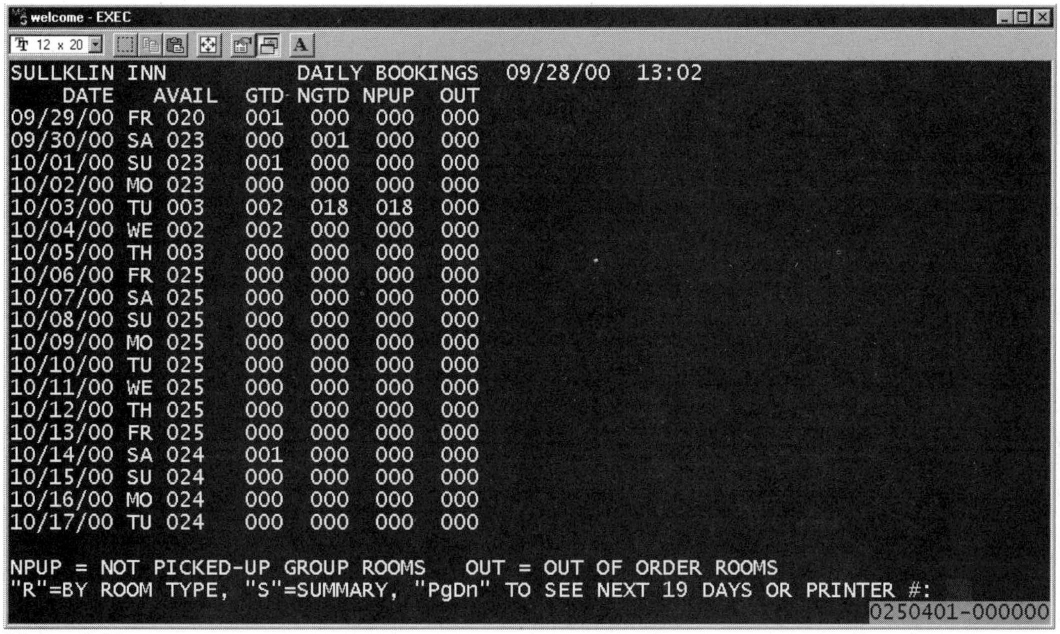

```
welcome - EXEC
12 x 20
SULLKLIN INN            DAILY BOOKINGS   09/28/00   13:02
    DATE    AVAIL   GTD  NGTD NPUP   OUT
09/29/00 FR 020    001  000  000   000
09/30/00 SA 023    000  001  000   000
10/01/00 SU 023    001  000  000   000
10/02/00 MO 023    000  000  000   000
10/03/00 TU 003    002  018  018   000
10/04/00 WE 002    002  000  000   000
10/05/00 TH 003    000  000  000   000
10/06/00 FR 025    000  000  000   000
10/07/00 SA 025    000  000  000   000
10/08/00 SU 025    000  000  000   000
10/09/00 MO 025    000  000  000   000
10/10/00 TU 025    000  000  000   000
10/11/00 WE 025    000  000  000   000
10/12/00 TH 025    000  000  000   000
10/13/00 FR 025    000  000  000   000
10/14/00 SA 024    001  000  000   000
10/15/00 SU 024    000  000  000   000
10/16/00 MO 024    000  000  000   000
10/17/00 TU 024    000  000  000   000

NPUP = NOT PICKED-UP GROUP ROOMS   OUT = OUT OF ORDER ROOMS
"R"=BY ROOM TYPE, "S"=SUMMARY, "PgDn" TO SEE NEXT 19 DAYS OR PRINTER #:
                                                        0250401-000000
```

**Figure 2.23**

Another screen used by management is the DAILY BOOKINGS screen. Management uses the DAILY BOOKINGS information to compare room availability by guaranteed, nonguaranteed, and group booking status. View this screen by pressing "R" for RESERVATIONS and H for DAILY BOOKINGS. Select tomorrow's date by pressing the F2 key.

Figure 2.23 shows the dates in the column on the left side of the screen, starting with tomorrow. Take note of the headings across the top of the table on the screen: AVAIL, GTD, NGTD, NPUP, and OUT.

The AVAIL column shows the total number of rooms available at the hotel for each date. GTD and NGTD represent guaranteed and nonguaranteed room reservations. Notice that on October 3, there are 2 guaranteed and 18 nonguaranteed reservations.

NPUP represents rooms on group blocks that have not been picked up. OUT represents the number of rooms that are out of order and not available to rent.

## Special Situations

What happens when two guests with different last names would like to reserve a room? This situation occurs fairly commonly when two adult guests, perhaps friends or colleagues, share a room. This is also the case when a husband and wife have different last names.

For example, in this example, a married couple who have different last names are sharing a room. To create this reservation, proceed by entering the information for the first guest, Mr. Lee Wong. Use the example in Figure 2.24 as your guide to enter the reservation information.

```
welcome - EXEC                                                            _ □ ×
T 12 x 20   □ □ □ □ □ □ A
ARRIVAL DATE: 08/23/01   THU                ADULT/CHILD: 2
NIGHTS: 002     DEPART: 08/25/01 SAT        ROOM TYPE:  KING
ID: 99 09/28  CHG:           GST TYPE: TRAN # OF ROOMS:     1
 SEGMENT: STND  TARIFF: RACK  PACKAGE:      RATE/RM:   10000

LAST NAME: WONG                      COMPANY: ORIENTAL CLASSIC IMPORTS
                                             CORP.#:
TITLE: MR       FIRST: LEE           GROUP:
                        HIST? N              GROUP#:
RESERVATION #: 00000659              RESV BY:
                                             PHONE:
                                     VIP?    #:        CLUB?    #:
***      GUEST ADDRESS      ***      TRAVEL AGENT #:
234 SOUTH THOMAS ST                  ** ADDITIONAL ADDRESS **
PHILADELPHIA, PA
                        19182
PHONE: 215-555-4444

GUARANTEED? Y   CREDIT CARD/CL #: 3788 8761 0088 8800
CONFIRM?    N                      ROLLOVER ROOM RATES? N
          DEPOSIT RECEIVED:                        HIST? N #1
COMMENTS:                                                 #2
                                                          #3
                                          0111201-000000
```

**Figure 2.24**

```
 welcome - EXEC                                                    _ □ ✕
 T 12 x 20 ▾
ARRIVAL DATE: 08/23/01   THU          ADULT/CHILD: 2
NIGHTS: 002    DEPART: 08/25/01 SAT   ROOM TYPE:  KING
ID: 99 09/28  CHG:          GST TYPE: TRAN    # OF ROOMS:    1
 SEGMENT: STND  TARIFF: RACK  PACKAGE:    RATE/RM:   10000

LAST NAME: _                          COMPANY: ORIENTAL CLASSIC IMPORTS

TITLE:          FIRST:         GROUP │ 1 = CHANGE ACCOMMODATIONS
                       HIST? N        │ 2 = CHANGE BASIC DATA
RESERVATION #: 00000659        RESV  │ 3 = CHANGE DEPOSIT DATA
                                      │ 4 = DISPLAY/CHANGE COMMENTS
                               VIP?  │ 5 = COPY RESERVATION
***    GUEST ADDRESS    ***    TRAVE │ 6 = BLOCK ROOM(S)
234 SOUTH THOMAS ST            ** AD │ 7 = UNBLOCK ROOM(S)
PHILADELPHIA, PA                      │ 8 = ENTER QUICK SHARE RES
                 19182                │ 9 = DISPLAY SHARES
PHONE: 215-555-4444                   │ U = UNSHARE RESERVATION
                                      │ A = PRINT REGISTRATION CARD
GUARANTEED? Y  CREDIT CARD/CL #: 3788 8761 00│ B = ENTER GOLF TEE-OFF TIME
CONFIRM?   N                  ROLLOVER RO│ C = AUTHORIZE CITY LEDGER
            DEPOSIT RECEIVED:         │ D = SHARE WITH ANOTHER RESV.
COMMENTS:
                                                        #3
*** ENTER NEW SHARE NAME
                                           0020520-000000
```

**Figure 2.25**

Since Mr. Wong is sharing a room with his wife, Mrs. Min Wu a reservation is made for her using a special procedure. From this screen select 8 (Figure 2.25) for ENTER QUICK SHARE RES. Enter Mrs. Min Wu's name on this screen. Press the Enter key then the Esc key to return to the main menu.

Go back into RESERVATIONS and display Mr. Wong's reservation; note that his reservation states that it is shared. The example in the workbook shows a circle around the words SHARE RESERVATION.

Congratulations, you have made a shared reservation.

The next special reservation function occurs when the hotel receives a deposit to guarantee a future reservation. This happens when the hotel receives payment in the form of a check, cash, money order, or other form of payment that must be recorded in the system.

For example, the hotel receives a check from April May, a guest who has a reservation for April 28, 2001. Her check is in the amount of $110.00, which is the first night's room rent plus tax. This will guarantee her reservation. First retrieve this reservation by pressing R for RESERVATIONS and 2 to display it (Figure 2.26). Enter the information to locate this particular reservation. If your reservation looks like the example, then you have located the correct reservation.

From the April May's reservation screen enter 3 to CHANGE DEPOSIT DATA. The deposit information is entered on this screen.

```
M welcome - EXEC                                                      _ □ ✕
T 12 x 20 ▾  ▣▤▧ ▨ ▧▤ A
ARRIVAL DATE: 04/28/01  SAT          ADULT/CHILD: 1
NIGHTS: 005  DEPARTING: 05/03/01  THU   ROOM TYPE:  KING
ID: 99 09/27  CHG: 99 09/27  GST TYPE: TRAN   # OF ROOMS:    1
 SEGMENT: STND  TARIFF: RACK  PACKAGE:   RATE/RM:   10000

LAST NAME: MAY                      COMPANY:

TITLE: MS      FIRST: APRIL      GROUP │ 1 = CHANGE ACCOMMODATIONS
                                       │ 2 = CHANGE BASIC DATA
RESERVATION #: 0000064C          RESV  │ 3 = CHANGE DEPOSIT DATA
                                       │ 4 = DISPLAY/CHANGE COMMENTS
                                 VIP?  │ 5 = COPY RESERVATION
***    GUEST ADDRESS    ***      TRAVE │ 6 = BLOCK ROOM(S)
900 SPRING GARDEN ST             ** AD │ 7 = UNBLOCK ROOM(S)
PHILADELPHIA, PA                       │ 8 = ENTER QUICK SHARE RES
                      19811            │ 9 = DISPLAY SHARES
PHONE: 215-555-8533                    │ U = UNSHARE RESERVATION
                                       │ A = PRINT REGISTRATION CARD
GUARANTEED?    CREDIT CARD/CL #:       │ B = ENTER GOLF TEE-OFF TIME
CONFIRM?   N              ROLLOVER RO  │ C = AUTHORIZE CITY LEDGER
          DEPOSIT RECEIVED:            │ D = SHARE WITH ANOTHER RESV.
COMMENTS: WILL MAIL DEPOSIT
                                                #3 0000
*** SELECT FUNCTION OR PRESS "ESC"         _        01612
                                       0231401-000000
```

**Figure 2.26**

Enter the information for this reservation (Figure 2.27). The payment was made in the form of a check, so either type "CK" or press F2. Enter your ID number and the amount of $110.00. In the AMOUNT field, enter the dollar amount as "11000" without a decimal point. Enter an N in the PRINT RECEIPT area. Congratulations, you have entered your first advance deposit.

```
M welcome - EXEC                                                      _ □ ✕
T 12 x 20 ▾  ▣▤▧ ▨ ▧▤ A
ARRIVAL DATE: 04/28/01  SAT          ADULT/CHILD: 1
NIGHTS: 005  DEPARTING: 05/03/01  THU   ROOM TYPE:  KING
ID: 99 09/27  CHG: 99 09/27  GST TYPE: TRAN   # OF ROOMS:    1
 SEGMENT: STND  TARIFF: RACK  PACKAGE:
                                             DEPOSITS
LAST NAME: MAY                      COMPA  REQUEST:
                                              ID:
TITLE: MS      FIRST: APRIL      GROUP        AMOUNT:    11000
                                              DUE BY DATE: 04/01/01
RESERVATION #: 0000064C      °   RESV
                                           RECEIVED:
                                 VIP?        PAYMENT TYPE: CK  ID: 99
***    GUEST ADDRESS    ***      TRAVE       AMOUNT:    11000
900 SPRING GARDEN ST             ** AD       DATE: 09/28/00
PHILADELPHIA, PA                             LAST CHNG DATE:  / /
                      19811
PHONE: 215-555-8533                        CHANGE:
                                              A = ADD, S = SUBTRACT
        ROOM    TAX    OCC   RM/TAX            AMOUNT:
 KING  500.00  50.00   .00  550.00 O          PAYMENT TYPE:    ID:
                                           PRINT RECEIPT?  _
       500.00  50.00   .00  550.00

                                       1070101-000000
```

**Figure 2.27**

## Chapter 2 Exercises

Name _____ Date _____

1) Enter a reservation for yourself. Use the arrival date of January 1, 2002. Request a suite.

2) After you have entered your reservation, view the ROOM AVAILIBILITY screen for January 1, 2002. Describe the impact your reservation has made to hotel's availability.

_____

_____

_____

_____

3) You receive a call from Nora Leahy. She would like a room on November 29. She lives at 14 Old Church Road, Silver Spring, Maryland, 20854.  During the reservation process, you discover that she had a reservation but cancelled it. Her plans have changed again and now she would like to rebook the reservation. Reactivate the cancelled reservation using the computer program; in this workbook ,describe the steps you took to make the change.
   a) What steps did you take to reactivate this room reservation for Ms. Leahy's room?

   _____

   _____

   b) What did you say to Ms. Leahy when helping her with this request to ensure that this transaction was handled accurately?

   _____

   _____

4) Two college roommates plan to take a road trip to Florida for spring break. The first stop on their trip is Wiley, Pennsylvania, and they plan to stay one night at your hotel. Joe Johnson and John Josephson want to share one room with two double beds on the night of March 10, 2001. Their address is 222 College Avenue, State College, Pennsylvania, 16804. The phone number is 814-555-1982. Offer these two guests the rack rate and make a reservation for them. They will use a Discover card to guarantee the reservation; the number is 6222 2323 9639 3693.
   a) What GUEST TYPE, SEGMENT, and TARIFF did you select for this reservation?

   _____

   b) What do you call two adults with different last names who will be staying in the same room?

   _____

5) The front desk just received a check in the amount of $110.00 for Mr. and Mrs. Harris Proud. They forgot to include the confirmation number in the letter that accompanied the check but they did include the arrival date of May 27, 2001.

   Locate the reservation and add the deposit information to the reservation record.
   a) What is the minimum amount of information you need to locate a reservation in the computer system?

   _____

6) Steven Biryani of the Daniels Energy Group is calling to make a reservation for the corporate meeting being held on hotel property. He plans to arrive on October 3, 2000, and stay for three nights. He doesn't care what bed type he gets, but he is requesting to be placed in a quiet part of the hotel. The Daniels Energy Company has a block of rooms in the hotel. Please book a room for Mr. Biryani from the block of rooms held by the Daniels Group.

   He lives at 16 Sherman Blvd., Apt. B, Atlanta, Georgia, 30081, and his work number is 770-555-1616.  He doesn't want to guarantee his room at this time.
   a) What is the difference between booking and blocking a room? How would you have reserved Mr. Biryani's room if he were *not* part of a group?

   _____

   _____

   _____

   _____

   _____

   b) How could you record Mr. Biryani's request to be placed in a quiet part of the hotel property?

   _____

   _____

7) A customer would like to book five rooms for two nights on September 30, 2000, and five rooms for two nights on October 5. They are not ready to reserve rooms at this time but would like information on what is available. Using the computer system, find out how many rooms are available for each situation and record the number of rooms and room type for each date.

   _____

   _____

8) How many rooms are due to check out on September 29, 2000? _____

9) How many rooms will be staying over on October 4, 2000? _____

10) What is the number of guaranteed room reservations for today? _____

11) Which screens did you use to find the information for questions 8, 9, and 10?

_____

_____

_____

_____

# CHAPTER 3

# REGISTRATION

## Key Learning Concepts in Chapter 3
- How to register a guest with a reservation.
- How to register a guest without a reservation (walk-in).
- How to find and change a reservation for a future date for someone who arrives today.
- What information to gather at registration.
- Steps to take in a normal registration process.

## What Is the Registration Process?

The registration, or check-in, process refers to the time the guest arrives at the property and is officially registered into the PMS. Several very simple circumstances will be covered in this chapter. They represent many of the common situations that will occur at guest registration. The registration process is also considered a key part of welcoming the guest to the property, because the tone and efficiency of the staff's handling of this process can go a long way to ensuring that the guest's stay is off to a good start. Well-trained staff, well-functioning equipment, and accurate reservation information are essential components of a good registration process.

### Registration Using Innstar

There are three possible cases for registration in Innstar. They are:

1. How to register a guest with a reservation.
2. How to register a guest without a reservation (walk-in).
3. How to find and change a reservation for a future date for someone who arrives today.

## How to Register a Guest with a Reservation.

In this case, a guest comes up to the registration desk and is greeted by the front desk staff person. As the guest identifies him- or herself, the front desk staff will search the registration list by selecting 1, CHECK IN WITH RESERVATION (Figure 3.1).

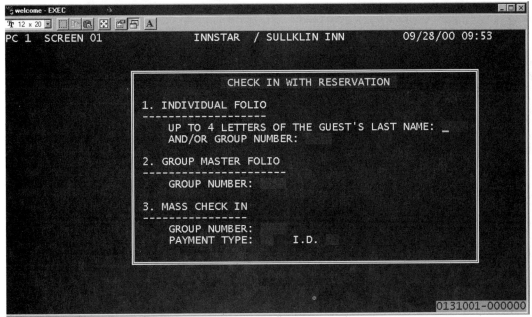

**Figure 3.1**

At this point, enter the first four letters of the last name of the guest; in this example, the guest has identified himself as John Adams, so type in the letters "ADAM"; then press the Page Down key to move to the next screen.

At this point, review the basic information with Mr. Adams to be sure you have found the correct reservation and that key information (length of stay, room type, spelling, etc.) is correct. In this example, we will assume the reservation is correct, so enter Y" in response to the question "CHECK IN THIS RESERVATION?" which appears at the bottom left of the screen (Figure 3.2).

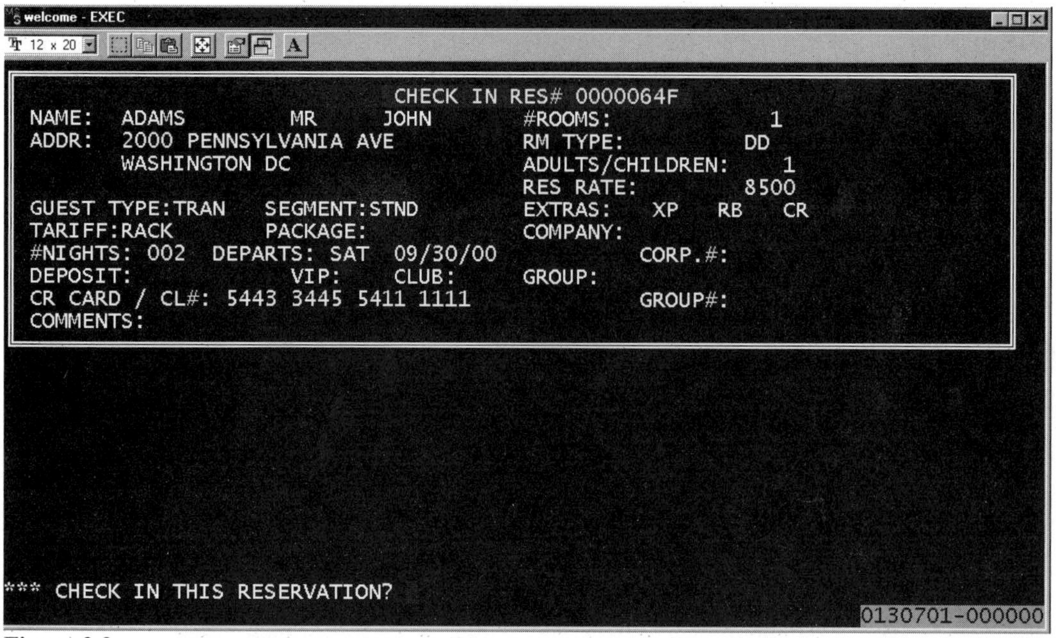

**Figure 3.2**

```
welcome - EXEC                                                    _ □ ×
T 12 x 20 ▾  ☐ ▯ ▤ ▣ ▤▤ A
                        CHECK IN RES# 0000064F
   NAME:   ADAMS       MR      JOHN      #ROOMS:           1
   ADDR:   2000 PENNSYLVANIA AVE         RM TYPE:          DD
           WASHINGTON DC                 ADULTS/CHILDREN:  1
                                         RES RATE:      8500
   GUEST TYPE:TRAN   SEGMENT:STND        EXTRAS:   XP   RB   CR
   TARIFF:RACK       PACKAGE:            COMPANY:
   #NIGHTS: 002  DEPARTS: SAT  09/30/00       CORP.#:
   DEPOSIT:         VIP:     CLUB:        GROUP:
   CR CARD / CL#: 5443 3445 5411 1111          GROUP#:
   COMMENTS:

   DD   101 I      85.00 PARK        DD   105 I      85.00 PARK
   DD   106 I      85.00 POOL        DD   109 I      85.00 PARK
   DD   200 I      85.00 POOL  SMOKE DD   203 I      85.00 PARK  SMOKE
   DD   205 I      85.00 PARK  SMOKE DD   206 I      85.00 POOL  SMOKE




                 SELECT ROOM # 1   _              (X=EXTRA)
                                                 0020520-000000
```

**Figure 3.3**

A list of available rooms that are ready for occupancy for the number of nights (shown as 002) for this reservation will appear on the screen (Figure 3.3). The "I" indicates a housekeeping status of "inspected," meaning that the room is ready for occupancy. Enter room "200" to proceed with this check-in.

When the next screen appears, enter "8500" for the FOLIO RATE, and "AX" for PAYMENT METHOD (Figure 3.4). This denotes an $85.00 room rate and American Express as the method of payment for this guest. In the CREDIT CARD/CITY LEDGER # field, enter

```
welcome - EXEC                                                    _ □ ×
T 12 x 20 ▾  ☐ ▯ ▤ ▣ ▤▤ A
                        CHECK IN
LAST NAME: ADAMS                      ROOM#:   200

TITLE: MR      FIRST: JOHN            ADULT/CHILD: 01/00

                                      EXTRAS:    XP    RB    CR

                                      RESV. RATE:   85.00

                                    ┌──────────────────────────┐
                                    │ ROOM        $   85.00    │
FOLIO RATE:    85.00(X=COMP)        │ RM TAX      $    8.50    │
PAYMENT METHOD:      MS             │ ADD. TAX    $     .00    │
CREDIT CARD/CITY LEDGER #:          │ NIGHTS           2      │
5443 3445 5411 1111                 │ TOTAL STAY$  187.00     │
                                    │ DEPOSIT     $     .00   │
ROLLOVER ROOM RATES? N              │ ────────                │
TAX NUMBER:                         │ DUE         $  187.00   │
                                    └──────────────────────────┘
YOUR I.D.:      _    PRE PAYMENT AMOUNT:         METHOD:

                                                 0170701-000000
```

**Figure 3.4**

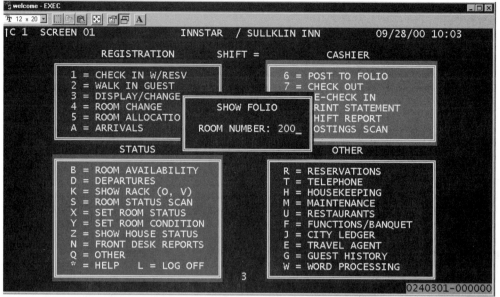

**Figure 3.5**

"5443 3445 5411 1111," then select N for the ROLLOVER ROOM RATES field; bypass the TAX NUMBER field by selecting Enter, then insert "01" in the YOUR I.D. field. At this point, the small box in the middle right of Figure 3.4 will appear showing the summary room rate and tax, totaling to the amount due. Depress the Page Down key to bypass additional questions, and enter N to not review the folio. Once completed, the system will return you to the main menu.

Let's verify that Mr. Adams is in room 200, by selecting 3, DISPLAY CHANGE FOLIO, and entering "200" in the room number field (Figure 3.5). Once you enter that number and select Enter, Figure 3.6 will appear.

Please review this screen, noting that it is the same Mr. Adams that we just registered into our property. Once we verify this, press the Esc key to return to the main menu.

```
 welcome - EXEC                                                        _ □ ×
 T 12 x 20   A
  ROOM TYPE: DD              SHOW FOLIO IN ROOM #  200    CURRENT RATE:   85.00
  FOLIO #: 0928-0012         DEPARTING: SAT  09/30/00
  NIGHTS LEFT: 002
  CREDIT LIMIT:    500.00    PAYMENT: MS          TARIFF: RACK
  ADULTS:  1  CHILDREN:      CR CARD / CL#: 5443 3445 5411 1111
  VIP: N #:        CLUB: N #:  COMPANY:
  TELE. CHARGES? N  RB:   CB:  CORP.#:
                             GROUP:
  LAST NAME:  ADAMS          GROUP #:
                             TAX NUMBER:
  TITLE: MR      FIRST: JOHN  TRAVEL AGENT#:
                             GUEST TYPE:    TRAN   HIST?   #1 0000
                             SEGMENT:       STND           #2 0000
  *** GUEST ADDRESS ***      ** ADDITIONAL ADDRESS **      #3 0000
  2000 PENNSYLVANIA AVE
  WASHINGTON DC
                    20019
     TELE#: 202-555-3232
     ROLLOVER ROOM RATES? N       MESSAGES - TEXT: N  VOICE: N
  COMMENTS:
  ----- CHECKED IN 09/28/00 09:56 BY ID: 99 --- RES ENTERED BY I.D.: 99
  * SELECT FUNCTION:   1 = CHANGE INFO    2 = STATEMENT    3 = RATE INFO
                       4 = COMMENTS  5 = GROUP BILLING PICKUP DEFINITIONS
                       6 = CREATE INCIDENTAL FOLIO  7 = AUTHORIZE C/L
                                                        0240101-000000
```

**Figure 3.6**

## How to Register a Guest without a Reservation (Walk-in)

When an incoming guest does not have a reservation, we have what most properties call a "walk-in" guest. Many properties welcome such additional business, but it is necessary to pay more attention to the creditworthiness of these guests. Innstar handles the guest without a reservation as 2, for WALK-IN GUEST. Select this option to see the screen shown in Figure 3.7.

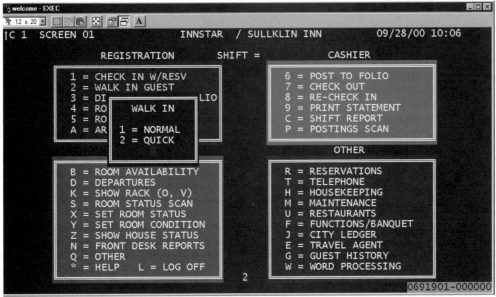

**Figure 3.7**

The system gives two options to proceed with this registration: to begin, select 1, NORMAL, and the screen shown in Figure 3.8 will appear.

This begins the process of walk-in registration, which essentially combines the check-in process with making a reservation for the guest. Enter the following information to complete this process.

NIGHTS: Enter 3; the screen in Figure 3.9 will appear to show the room availability by room type and rate for number of days the guest plans to stay at the property.

Press any key to continue to the next screen.

```
 welcome - EXEC                                                          _ □ ×
 T 12 x 20                A
WALK IN REGISTRATION              INNSTAR   / SULLKLIN INN        09/28/00 10:07

NIGHTS: 3
    OR DEPARTURE DATE:     /  /
```

**Figure 3.8**

```
 welcome - EXEC                                                          _ □ ×
 T 12 x 20                A
WALK IN REGISTRATION              INNSTAR   / SULLKLIN INN        09/28/00 10:07

NIGHTS:    3
       DEPARTING: 10/01/00  SUN

SEP 00 28    29    30    01    02    03   04      28     29     30     01     02     03
       THU   FRI   SAT   SUN   MON   TUE  WED     THU    FRI    SAT    SUN    MON    TUE
DD      8     9    10    10    10          1-    8500   8500   8500   8500   8500   8500
KING    5     8    10    10    10               10000  10000  10000  10000  10000  10000
SUIT    3     3     3     3     3     3    3




AVAIL  16    20    23    23    23     3    2
*** ANY KEY TO CONTINUE                                            0302501-010000
```

**Figure 3.9**

```
welcome - EXEC                                                    _ □ ×
T 12 x 20 ▾ 
WALK IN REGISTRATION              INNSTAR  / SULLKLIN INN       09/28/00 10:10

NIGHTS:   3                            ADULTS:      CHILDREN:
     DEPARTING: 10/01/00  SUN          EXTRAS:  XP   RB   CR
LAST NAME:                             COMPANY:
TITLE:          FIRST:                            CORP.#:
                 SEARCH HISTORY? N     GROUP:
GUEST TYPE:       SEGMENT:                      GROUP#:
TARIFF:           PACKAGE:
***     GUEST ADDRESS       ***        ** ADDITIONAL ADDRESS **



PHONE:    -                            VIP?  #:        CLUB?  #:

COMMENTS:






                                                         0020520-000000
```

**Figure 3.10**

Proceed to enter the reservation data as you have in past lessons using the information indicated in Figure 3.10. Ms. Tanaka's address is 7 Lucky Drive in Atlantic City, New Jersey, 08401. Her phone number is 609-555-8888. At the end of the COMMENTS field, press Enter.

Figure 3.11 shows the rooms that are available and ready for sale. Enter "106" for Ms Tanaka; this is a DD room at $85.00 per night. Figure 3.12 shows the same check-in completion screen that we saw earlier in this lesson; enter the data as indicated next.

```
welcome - EXEC                                                    _ □ ×
T 12 x 20 ▾ 
WALK IN REGISTRATION              INNSTAR  / SULLKLIN INN       09/28/00 11:03

NIGHTS:   3                            ADULTS: 1    CHILDREN:
     DEPARTING: 10/01/00  SUN          EXTRAS:  XP   RB   CR
LAST NAME: TANAKA                      COMPANY:
TITLE: MS        FIRST: YUKI                      CORP.#:
                 SEARCH HISTORY? N     GROUP:
GUEST TYPE: TRAN  SEGMENT: STND                 GROUP#:
TARIFF: RACK      PACKAGE:
***     GUEST ADDRESS       ***        ** ADDITIONAL ADDRESS **
7 LUCKY DRIVE
ATLANTIC CITY NJ
DD      101 I       85.00 PARK         KING   102 I    100.00 POOL
DD      105 I       85.00 PARK         DD     106 I     85.00 POOL
KING    107 I      100.00 PARK         DD     109 I     85.00 PARK
DD      203 I       85.00 PARK  SMOKE  DD     205 I     85.00 PARK   SMOKE
DD      206 I       85.00 POOL  SMOKE  KING   207 I    100.00 PARK   SMOKE
SUIT    300 I             PARK         KING   301 I    100.00 POOL
SUIT    302 I             PARK         SUIT   304 I           PARK
KING    303 D      100.00 POOL

                    SELECT ROOM # 1
                                                         0302601-000100
```

**Figure 3.11**

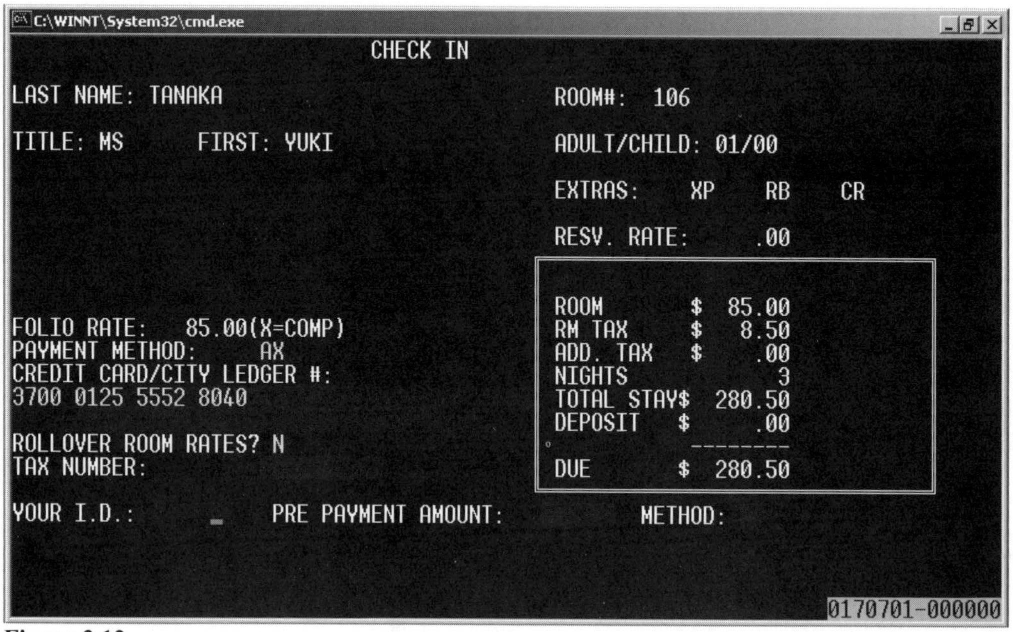

**Figure 3.12**

As you compete the folio, respond N to the question REVIEW FOLIO?, and the system will return to the main menu. Again select 3, DISPLAY CHANGE FOLIO, to verify that Ms. Tanaka is registered in Room 106 (Figure 3.13). If this is correct, press the Esc key to return to the main menu.

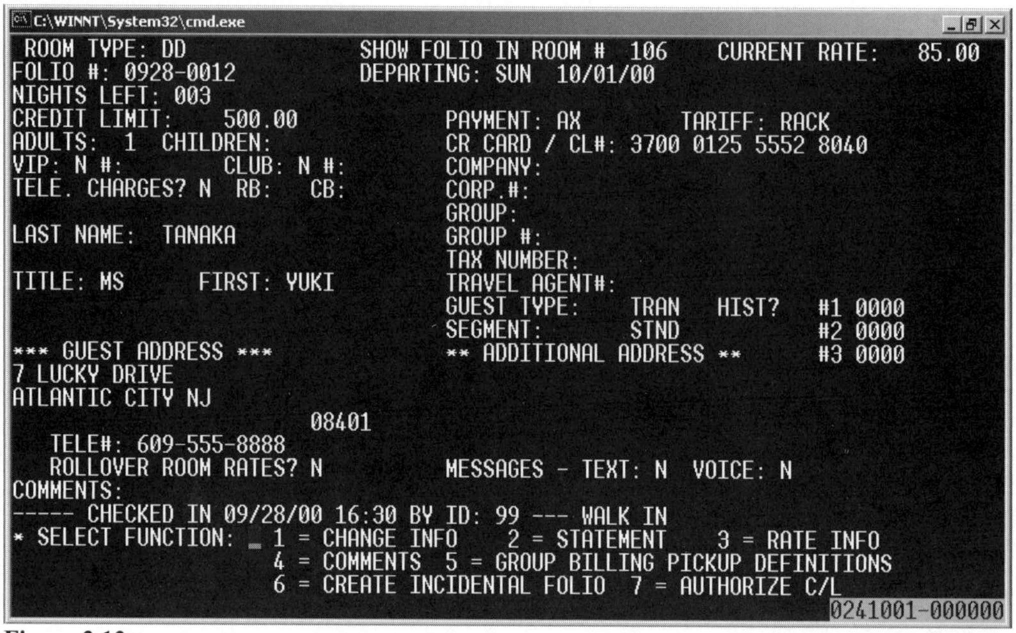

**Figure 3.13**

## How to Find and Change a Reservation for a Future Date for a Guest Who Arrives Today

In some cases, a guest may come to the registration desk with a reservation, but for a date in the future. If we registered the guest based on room availability, we can change the reservation date of arrival to today's date, then proceed with a normal registration from that point on. Let's work through an example. Mr. Jorge Estrada arrives the registration desk to check in and says that he has a reservation; but it does not show up when we initially select 1, for CHECK-IN W/RESV option. At this point, we go to Innstar's RESERVATIONS functions by selecting R. The screen shown in Figure 3.14 appears.

Select 2, for DISPLAY / CHANGE, and enter the letters "EST" in the name field, then press the Page Down key (Figure 3.15).

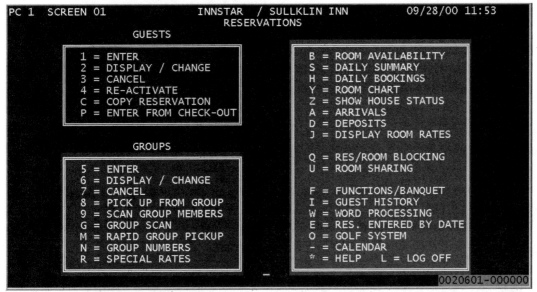

**Figure 3.14**

```
ARRIVAL DATE: 10/01/00  SUN          ADULT/CHILD: 1
NIGHTS: 004  DEPARTING: 10/05/00  THU  ROOM TYPE:  KING
ID: 99 09/27  CHG: 00        GST TYPE: TRAN  # OF ROOMS:    1
 SEGMENT: STND  TARIFF: RACK  PACKAGE:     RATE/RM:   10000

LAST NAME: ESTRADA                    COMPANY: THREE STAR TRUCKING
                                               CORP.#:
TITLE: MR       FIRST: JORGE          GROUP:
                                               GROUP#:
RESERVATION #: 00000650               RESV BY: SECRETARY
                                               PHONE:
                                      VIP?  #:         CLUB?  #:
***     GUEST ADDRESS     ***         TRAVEL AGENT #:
100 BAYSIDE DR                        ** ADDITIONAL ADDRESS **
MIAMI FL
                        33138
PHONE: 305-555-8978

GUARANTEED? Y  CREDIT CARD/CL #: 3456 2445 3456 2222      C/L AUTH.: N
CONFIRM?   N                ROLLOVER ROOM RATES? N
            DEPOSIT RECEIVED:                        HIST?   #1 0000
COMMENTS:                                                    #2 0000
                                                             #3 0000
*** DISPLAY/CHANGE THIS RESERVATION?  (Y OR N)                 01616
                                                      0230501-010000
```

**Figure 3.15**

```
welcome - EXEC                                                    _ □ ×
T 12 x 20 ▼   □□□ ⊠ □□ A
  ROOM TYPE: KING          SHOW FOLIO IN ROOM #  301   CURRENT RATE:  100.00
FOLIO #: 0928-0014         DEPARTING: MON  10/02/00
NIGHTS LEFT: 004
CREDIT LIMIT:     500.00   PAYMENT: AX        TARIFF: RACK
ADULTS:  1  CHILDREN:      CR CARD / CL#: 3456 2445 3456 2222
VIP: N #:        CLUB: N #:  COMPANY:         THREE STAR TRUCKING
TELE. CHARGES? N  RB:   CB:  CORP.#:
                           GROUP:
LAST NAME:  ESTRADA        GROUP #:
                           TAX NUMBER:
TITLE: MR       FIRST: JORGE  TRAVEL AGENT#:
                           GUEST TYPE:    TRAN   HIST?   #1 0000
                           SEGMENT:       STND           #2 0000
*** GUEST ADDRESS ***      ** ADDITIONAL ADDRESS **      #3 0000
100 BAYSIDE DR
MIAMI FL
                  33138
  TELE#: 305-555-8978
  ROLLOVER ROOM RATES? N         MESSAGES - TEXT: N  VOICE: N
COMMENTS:
----- CHECKED IN 09/28/00 11:57 BY ID: 99 --- RES ENTERED BY I.D.: 99
* SELECT FUNCTION: _ 1 = CHANGE INFO    2 = STATEMENT    3 = RATE INFO
              4 = COMMENTS  5 = GROUP BILLING PICKUP DEFINITIONS
              6 = CREATE INCIDENTAL FOLIO  7 = AUTHORIZE C/L
                                                      0241001-000000
```

**Figure 3.16**

Enter Y, for yes, because this is the reservation we want; select 1, for the CHANGE ACCOMMODATIONS option in the box.  After pressing "," you may make changes to the screen (Figure 3.16). This will permit you to change the date of arrival from October 1, 2000, to today's date, in this case, September 28, 2000.  Once you have made that change. press the Page Down key until you return to the main menu, since no other changes to the reservation are required at this time. Again select1, for CHECK-IN W/RESV, and proceed to check in Mr. Estrada as you have done earlier in this chapter.

## Chapter 3 Exercises

Name _____ Date _____

1) In the previous chapter, you made a reservation for yourself on January 1, 2002. Change the arrival date to today.

2) Check in your reservation and put yourself in the suite.

3) Tony and Tina Tourmaline do not have a reservation, but would like a room near the pool. They plan to stay one night and want to pay cash for the room. Register this couple and collect the correct amount of money.
   a) How do you determine which rooms are located by the pool?

   _____

   _____

   b) How much cash should you collect and why?

   _____

   _____

   _____

   _____

4) A man walks up to the front desk and explains that he thinks he has a reservation for September 29. His plans have changed and he is here now. His says his name is Nelson Thomas and he would like a room for two nights. Check him in.
   a) What steps did you take to accommodate this guest?

   _____

   _____

   _____

   _____

   _____

   _____

   _____

5) Peter Murky of Precision Data Collection (PDC) Corp. would like a room for one night, and he requests a corporate rate. The corporate rate for PDC Corp. is $10 off the rack rate. Mr. Murky does not have a reservation, so he provides his work address and phone number. PDC is located at 999 Rainforest Rd, Portland, Oregon 97206. His work number is 503-555-9999. He uses his American Express card, number 3747 9999 9511 1159, to pay for the room.
   a)   What room rate did you give Mr. Murky?_____

6) Hy Roller would like a room with a king bed. He would like to use his Visa card to check in but he informs you that he will pay cash at check-out. His address is 80 Baccarat Way, Las Vegas, Nevada, 89103. He refuses to give his phone number. His Visa card number is 4444 7391 1793 8528.
   a)   How would you handle this guest at check-in?

   _____

   _____

   _____

   _____

   _____

7) Check the room availability screen by pressing the B key. For today's date, what is availability for each room type and for the entire property for today?

   _____

   _____

   _____

   _____

8) What is the occupancy percentage for today? As the hotel owner, how do you feel about this level of occupancy?

   _____

   _____

   _____

   _____

# CHAPTER 4

## POSTING AND FOLIO MANAGEMENT

### Key Learning Concepts in Chapter 4
- How to post to a folio directly from PM.
- How to post to a folio via an interface.
- How to correct a posting.
- How to transfer a posting.
- How to do a check-out.
- How to do cashier end-of-shift reporting.

### Posting to a Folio Directly from the PMS

While many postings to folios in a typical PMS will occur via interfaces (such as the interface to the point-of-sale dining system or the telephone call accounting system), the same basic posting data can be entered directly from the PMS. Innstar provides a very simple process to post a charge or payment item to a folio. Let's do a few postings to demonstrate the proper means of posting to an in-house folio.

From the main screen, select 6 from the CASHIER BOX; you will see the screen shown in Figure 4.1.

```
welcome - EXEC                                                    _ □ ×
 T 12 x 20    ▢ ▣ ▣ ▣ ▣ ▣ A

                    ┌─────────────────────────────┐
                    │        FOLIO POST           │
                    │                             │
                    │   ROOM NUMBER: _            │
                    │                             │
                    │   1 = NEW POSTING           │
                    │   2 = CORRECTION            │
                    │   3 = ADJUSTMENT            │
                    │   4 = XFER 1 POSTING        │
                    │   5 = BALANCE XFER          │
                    │   6 = CLASS XFER            │
                    │                             │
                    │                             │
                    │   + = CHARGE                │
                    │   - = CREDIT                │
                    │                             │
                    └─────────────────────────────┘

                                                    0250402-000000
```

Figure 4.1

Enter room 201, as it is occupied; then select 1, for NEW POSTING, then the plus sign (+) for CHARGE (Figure 4.2).

The options above the postings list types currently in the system. Select 12, for LOCAL TELE, so we can post a local telephone call directly from this screen. The screen in Figure 4.3 will appear.

Enter "1.20" for the POSTING AMOUNT, enter "123" for the REFERENCE NUMBER, enter "local" for the REFERENCE COMMENT field, and finally enter "01" in the YOUR ID field. As you complete entry of the ID field, the posting will occur and you will return to the screen shown in Figure 4.4. Notice at the bottom of the screen the message "POST DONE!"

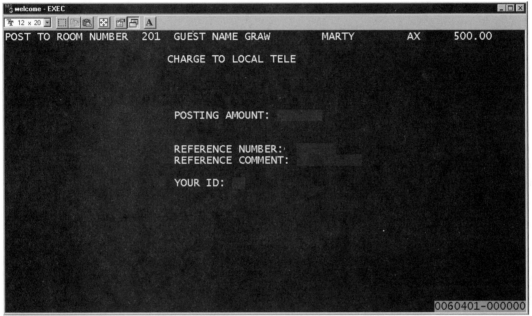

Figure 4.2

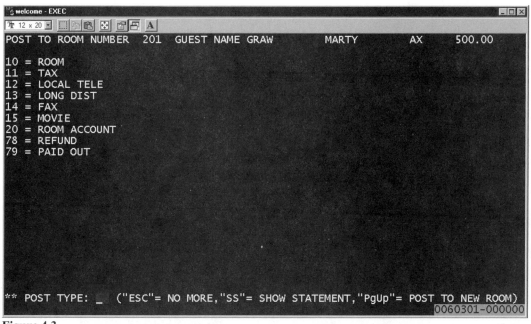

**Figure 4.3**

**Figure 4.4**

This will allow another posting in a rapid manner. We will now post a fax charge to the folio. To begin, select 14 for a FAX posting, enter "5.00" for the posting amount, and then enter "505" for the REFERENCE NUMBER, and "HOME" for the REFERENCE COMMENT, as shown in Figure 4.5.

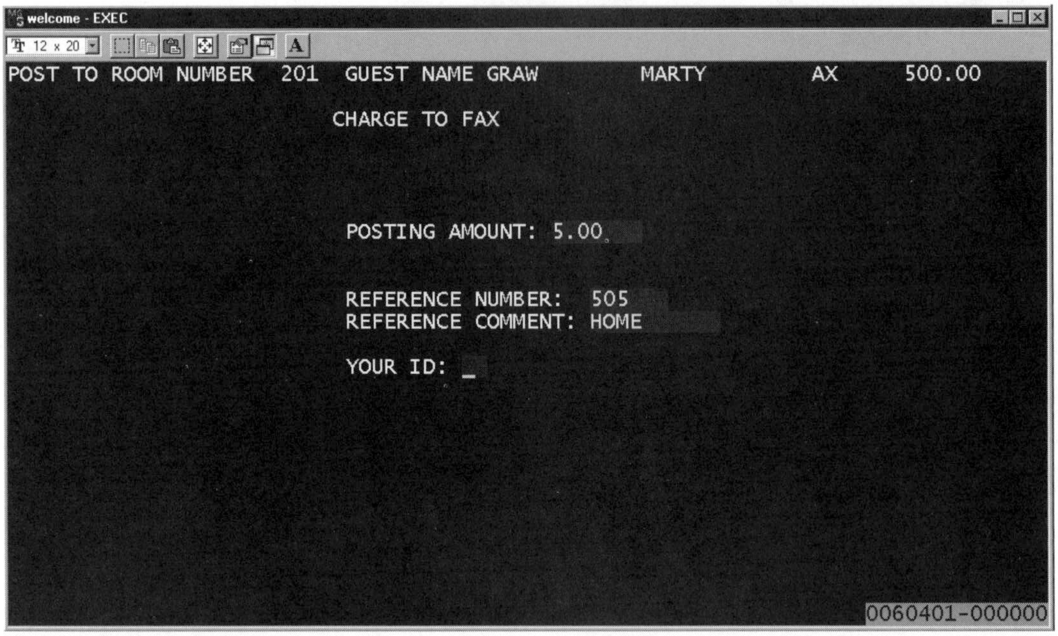

**Figure 4.5**

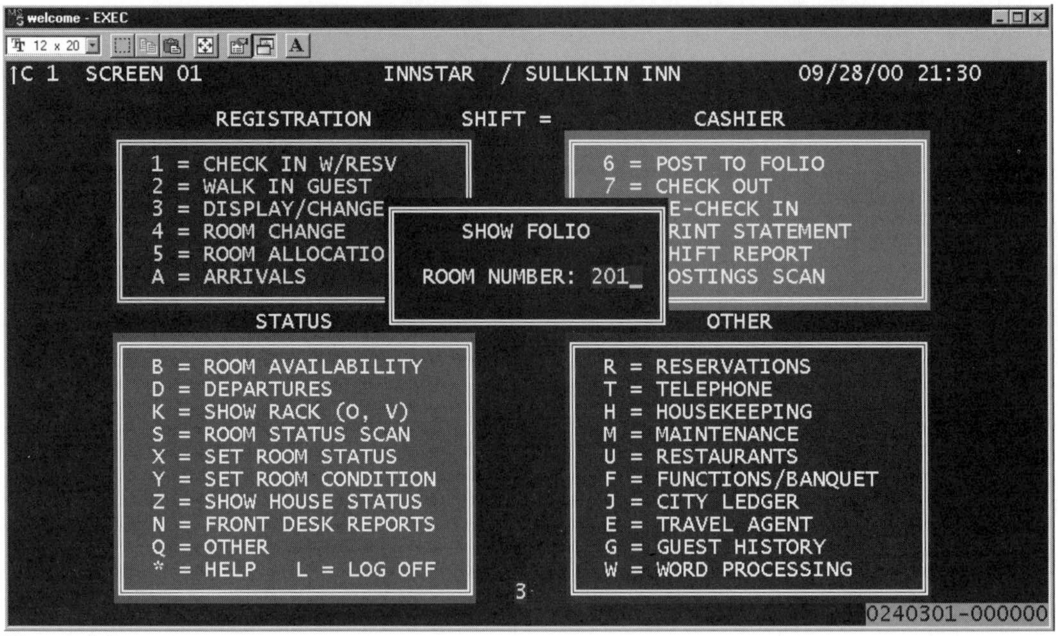

**Figure 4.6**

Complete this posting by entering your ID number in the YOUR ID field. These two postings can be reviewed by returning to the main screen, selecting 3, DISPLAY CHANGE FOLIO, then "201" for the room number, as shown in Figure 4.6. Figure 4.7 shows the folio.

```
welcome - EXEC                                                    _ □ ×
T 12 x 20 ▼  □ □ □ □ □ □ A
  ROOM TYPE: KING          SHOW FOLIO IN ROOM #  201   CURRENT RATE:   85.00
 FOLIO #: 0927-0008        DEPARTING: SAT  09/30/00
 NIGHTS LEFT: 002          PREVIOUS RM#:  200
 CREDIT LIMIT:    500.00   PAYMENT: AX       TARIFF: RACK
 ADULTS:  1  CHILDREN:     CR CARD / CL#: 3766 8880 2323 0001
 VIP: N #:        CLUB: N #:   COMPANY:      YUMMY FOODS INC
 TELE. CHARGES? N  RB:   CB:   CORP.#:
                          GROUP:
 LAST NAME:  GRAW         GROUP #:
                          TAX NUMBER:
 TITLE: MR       FIRST: MARTY   TRAVEL AGENT#:
                          GUEST TYPE:    TRAN   HIST?   #1 0000
                          SEGMENT:       STND           #2 0000
 *** GUEST ADDRESS ***    ** ADDITIONAL ADDRESS **      #3 0000
 32 BOURBON ST
 NEW ORLEANS LA
                   70115
    TELE#: 504-555-8711
    ROLLOVER ROOM RATES? N        MESSAGES - TEXT: N  VOICE: N
 COMMENTS:
 ----- CHECKED IN 09/27/00 23:16 BY ID: 99 --- WALK IN
 * SELECT FUNCTION:   1 = CHANGE INFO    2 = STATEMENT    3 = RATE INFO
                      4 = COMMENTS  5 = GROUP BILLING PICKUP DEFINITIONS
                      6 = CREATE INCIDENTAL FOLIO  7 = AUTHORIZE C/L
                                                        0240101-000000
```

**Figure 4.7**

```
welcome - EXEC                                                    _ □ ×
T 12 x 20 ▼  □ □ □ □ □ □ A
                         STATEMENT
 ROOM:  201  GUEST: GRAW        PAY METHOD & LIMIT: AX   500.00  PERS: 01

 NO.   DATE    REF    DESCRIPTION      COMMENT      AMOUNT      ID

  1.  09/27      1   ROOM                            85.00   SYSTEM
  2.  09/27          TAX                              8.50   SYSTEM
  3.  09/28    123   LOCAL TELE      LOCAL            1.20   99
  4.  09/28    505   FAX             HOME             5.00   99
                     *** BALANCE ***                99.70




 **** (SPACE = CONTINUE)  or PgUp for Prev Page
                                                        0640101-000000
```

**Figure 4.8**

There are several options for reviewing FOLIO information. First, select 2 for STATEMENT, and the screen shown in Figure 4.8 will appear.

This will show the two recent postings for the LOCAL TELEPHONE and FAX charges. Return to the main screen by pressing the Esc key. Let's begin to make a payment to the same folio by selecting 6, for POSTING, and entering room "201. Next select 1, for NEW POSTING, then enter a dash (—) for CREDIT. The screen shown in Figure 4.9 will appear.

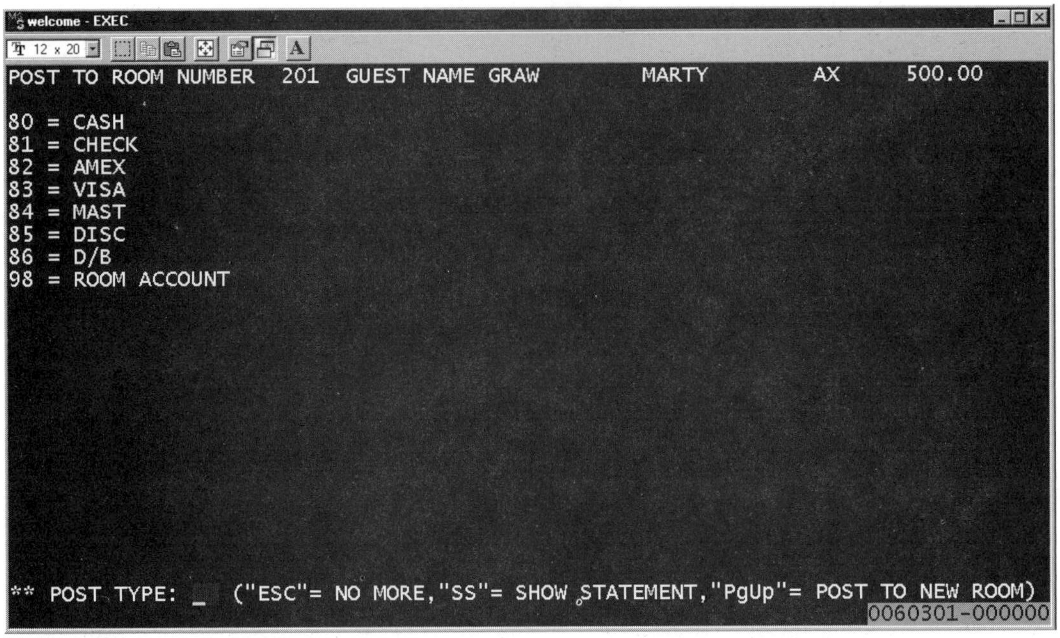

```
welcome - EXEC                                                    _ □ ✕
 T 12 x 20 ▾  ☐ ▣▣ ☒ ☐▤ A
POST TO ROOM NUMBER   201   GUEST NAME GRAW       MARTY      AX      500.00

80 = CASH
81 = CHECK
82 = AMEX
83 = VISA
84 = MAST
85 = DISC
86 = D/B
98 = ROOM ACCOUNT




** POST TYPE: _  ("ESC"= NO MORE,"SS"= SHOW STATEMENT,"PgUp"= POST TO NEW ROOM)
                                                        0060301-000000
```

**Figure 4.9**

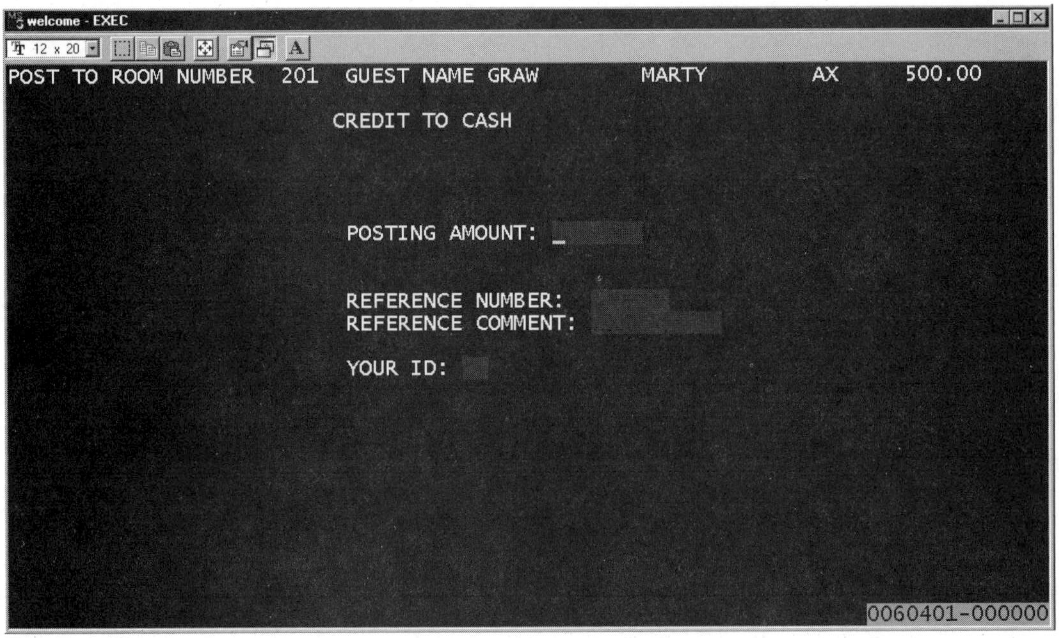

```
welcome - EXEC                                                    _ □ ✕
 T 12 x 20 ▾  ☐ ▣▣ ☒ ☐▤ A
POST TO ROOM NUMBER   201   GUEST NAME GRAW       MARTY      AX      500.00

            CREDIT TO CASH



            POSTING AMOUNT: _


            REFERENCE NUMBER:
            REFERENCE COMMENT:

            YOUR ID:




                                                        0060401-000000
```

**Figure 4.10**

We will make a cash payment to this account, so enter "80" to indicate the method of payment (see Figure 4.10). Enter "100.00" for the POSTING AMOUNT, next "201" for the REFERENCE NUMBER, and then "cash" for the REFERENCE COMMENT; finally, enter your ID number in the YOUR ID field. After that posting is done, the posting screen will reappear.

Now we will post a check payment, so enter "81" for CHECK and the screen in Figure 4.11 will appear.

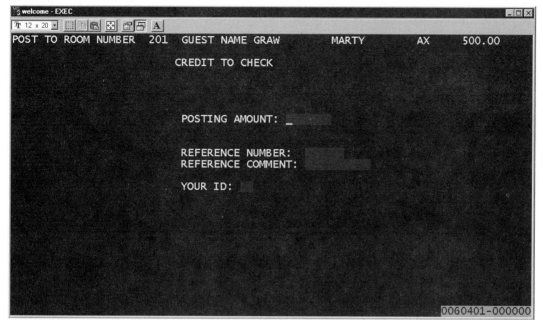

**Figure 4.11**

```
welcome - EXEC                                                    _ □ ×
T 12 x 20 ▼
                        STATEMENT
ROOM:  201   GUEST: GRAW       PAY METHOD & LIMIT: AX   500.00  PERS: 01

NO.   DATE    REF    DESCRIPTION       COMMENT      AMOUNT    ID

 1.  09/27      1    ROOM                            85.00    SYSTEM
 2.  09/27           TAX                              8.50    SYSTEM
 3.  09/28    123    LOCAL TELE        LOCAL          1.20    99
 4.  09/28    505    FAX               HOME           5.00    99
 5.  09/28    201    CASH              CASH         100.00CR  99
 6.  09/28    101    CHECK             CHECK 16      50.00CR  99
                     *** BALANCE ***                50.30CR




**** (SPACE = CONTINUE)  or PgUp for Prev Page
                                                   0640101-000000
```

**Figure 4.12**

Enter "50.00" for the POSTING AMOUNT, then "101" for the REFERENCE NUMBER, then "Check 16" for the REFERENCE COMMENT; finally, enter "01" in the YOUR ID: field. This will complete the two payment postings.

Let's look at the folio to be sure we posted the payments properly. Return to the main screen and select option 3 for DISPLAY CHANGE FOLIO; enter "201" for the ROOM NUMBER, then select option 2 for STATEMENT. The screen in Figure 4.12 will appear showing the two payments.

## Posting to a Folio via an Interface

In today's PMS environment, interfaces to many revenue-producing systems are commonplace. The Telephone Call Accounting and Restaurant Point-of-Sale interfaces are most common, and handle the largest number of transactions. Since each of these interfaces is written to serve the specific system that is being connected, it is impossible to demonstrate the interfaces here. The primary reason for the interface is to facilitate posting from one system to the PMS, thus eliminating the need to do this manually, as we have done in our examples. Labor savings, speed of posting, and accuracy are the benefits of a properly functioning interface environment.

As you operate PMS systems in the "real world," you will get first-hand knowledge of both the benefits generated and the issues raised by interfaces. One key to working with these interfaces is to recognize that most systems allow the same type of posting to be done manually in the event the interface is not installed or is not functioning properly. Other common interfaces, both revenue-producing and operational, are:

- Movies
- Internet Access
- Central Reservations Systems
- Telephone PBX
- Energy Management
- Security and Fire Safety
- Sales and Catering
- Guest Room Locking System
- Credit

## Correction to a Posting

When an error is made in the posting process, you will need to know how to make a correction to the posting made to a guest room folio. Key to the audit control is to be sure that the correction is properly documented and that any change to the guest folio is made accurately and in a timely manner. As an example of how Innstar handles the process, we will make a correction to a posting that we just made to Room 201.

Let's change the posting for the FAX, which we entered as $5.00, to $6.00. To do this from the main screen, 6, for POST TO FOLIO; enter room "201," then select 2, for CORRECTION, and then the plus (+) key because we are going to add to the posting. The screen will appear as shown in Figure 4.13. As you enter the plus (+) sign, a subsequent screen will appear, showing the current folio statement for the guest in room 201.

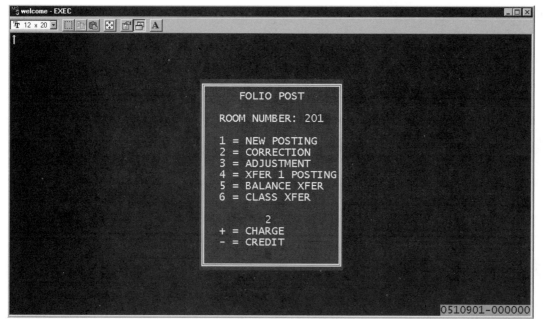

**Figure 4.13**

```
welcome - EXEC                                                    _ □ ×
 T 12 x 20                 A

                STATEMENT
ROOM:  201  GUEST: GRAW        PAY METHOD & LIMIT: AX   500.00  PERS: 01

NO.   DATE      REF    DESCRIPTION      COMMENT      AMOUNT    ID

 1.  09/27       1    ROOM                            85.00   SYSTEM
 2.  09/27            TAX                              8.50   SYSTEM
 3.  09/28      123   LOCAL TELE        LOCAL          1.20   99
 4.  09/28      505   FAX               HOME           5.00   99
 5.  09/28      201   CASH              CASH        100.00CR  99
 6.  09/28      101   CHECK             CHECK 16     50.00CR  99
     NO MORE




***  SELECT  RELATED  POSTING:  4_   or PgUp for Prev Page
                                                      0020520-000000
```

**Figure 4.14**

In the SELECT RELATED POSTING field, enter 4 to correspond to the posting for the FAX charge that we made earlier. This will result in the screen shown in Figure 4.14.

Enter "1.00" in the POSTING AMOUNT field (this is the additional charge that we need to bring the total to $6.00); in the COMMENT FIELD, enter "ERROR," then your two digit ID number in YOUR ID field, as in Figure 4.15.

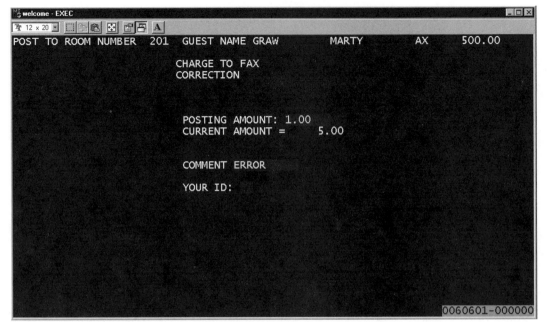

**Figure 4.15**

```
welcome - EXEC                                                        _ □ ×
 T 12 x 20                          A
                               STATEMENT
ROOM:  201  GUEST: GRAW          PAY METHOD & LIMIT: AX   500.00  PERS: 01

NO.  DATE    REF   DESCRIPTION         COMMENT      AMOUNT     ID

  1.  09/27     1   ROOM                             85.00     SYSTEM
  2.  09/27         TAX                               8.50     SYSTEM
  3.  09/28   123   LOCAL TELE          LOCAL         1.20     99
  4.  09/28   505   FAX                 HOME          5.00     99
  5.  09/28   201   CASH                CASH        100.00CR   99
  6.  09/28   101   CHECK               CHECK 16     50.00CR   99
  7.  09/28   505   FAX          CORR   ERROR         1.00     99
             *** BALANCE ***                         49.30CR

**** (SPACE = CONTINUE)  or PgUp for Prev Page
                                                    0640101-000000
```

**Figure 4.16**

As you enter your ID in the YOUR ID field, the posting will complete. To verify the posting change, return to the main screen and select 3, DISPLAY CHANGE FOLIO, enter "201," and select 2, for STATEMENT, to show the current statement. Notice the entry for $1.00 that corresponds to the original posting of $5.00 for the FAX (Figure 4.16).

## Transfer of a Posting

To deal with the case of a posting that has been made to a different folio than the one intended, the PMS has a TRANSFER function that allows moving the posting from one folio to another. We will look at how Innstar handles this common transaction.

The posting that we want to transfer is the LOCAL TELE charge on the folio of room 201:  we want to move that to room 200, the folio of another guest. From the main screen, select 6, POST TO FOLIO, enter room 201, then select 4, XFER 1 POSTING ( short for transfer one posting), and then (+) See Figure 4.17.

When the current folio statement for room 201 displays, select item 3, for the LOCAL TELEPHONE charge. The screen shown in Figure 4.18 is where you select that posting.

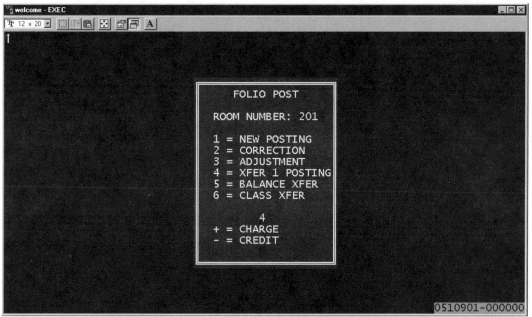

**Figure 4.17**

```
                          STATEMENT
ROOM:  201   GUEST: GRAW         PAY METHOD & LIMIT: AX   500.00   PERS: 01

NO.    DATE      REF    DESCRIPTION      COMMENT      AMOUNT     ID

 1.   09/27       1     ROOM                           85.00    SYSTEM
 2.   09/27             TAX                             8.50    SYSTEM
 3.   09/28      123    LOCAL TELE       LOCAL          1.20    99
 4.   09/28      505    FAX              HOME           5.00    99
 5.   09/28      201    CASH             CASH        100.00CR   99
 6.   09/28      101    CHECK            CHECK 16     50.00CR   99
      NO MORE




SELECT RELATED POSTING: 3   (PgUp for Prev Page) ENTER AMOUNT IF PARTIAL:
```

**Figure 4.18**

Press Enter twice to skip the ENTER AMOUNT IF PARTIAL field on the bottom right of screen. When the next screen appears, enter room "200" as the room folio to which we are transferring the charge, and put your ID number in the YOUR ID field, as shown in Figure 4.19.

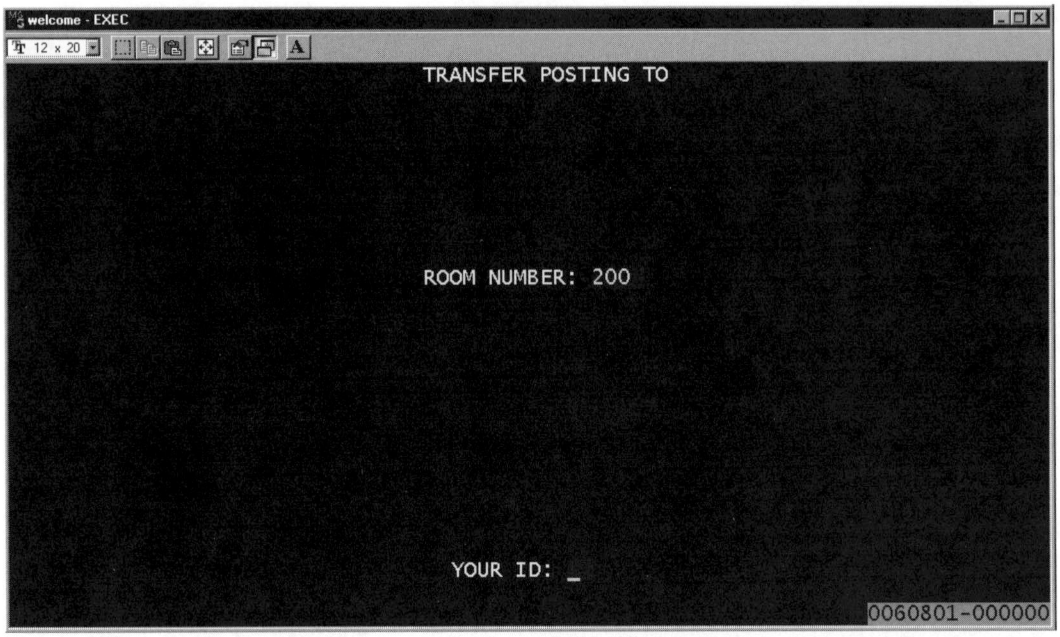

**Figure 4.19**

To verify this transaction, from the main screen, select 3, for DISPLAY CHANGE FOLIO, enter room "200" (Figure 4.19), then select 2 to review the statement; it will appear as in Figure 4.20, showing the posting

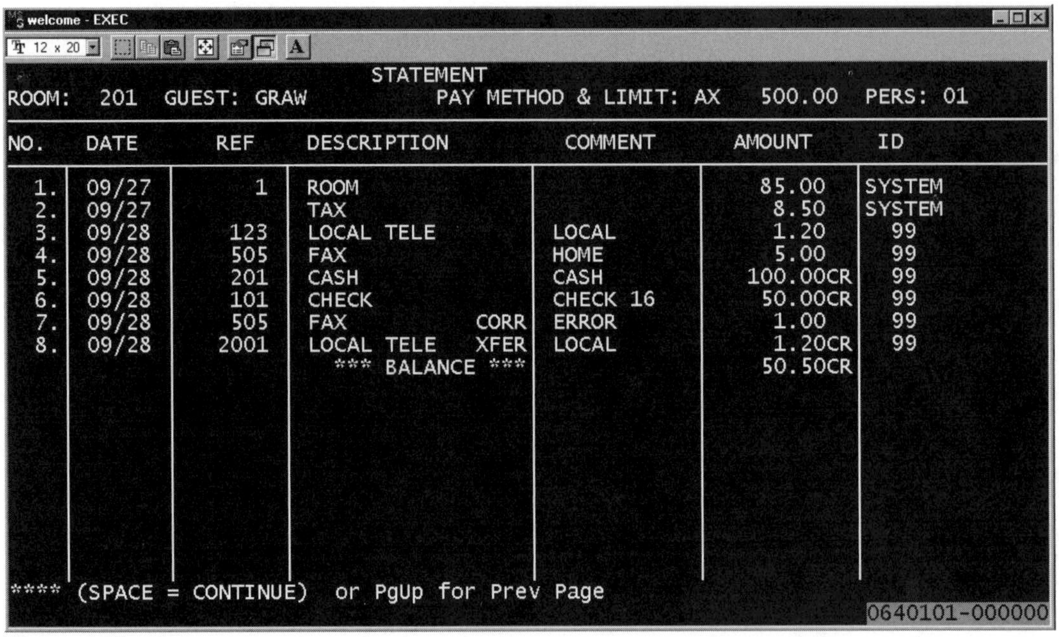

**Figure 4.20**

Repeat that process for room 201 to show the other end of the transaction (Figure 4.21).

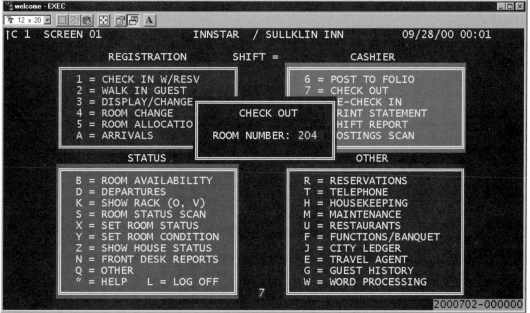

**Figure 4.21**

## Check-out

As guests complete their stay at the Sullklin Inn, they will request a check-out. There are several ways to check out a guest using modern PMS technology, but we will choose the traditional one that Innstar supports. From the main screen, select option 7, CHECK-OUT, to begin the process. In our example, we will check out Ms. Dottie Colm in room 204. After you select option 7 and enter room 204, the screen shown in Figure 4.22 will appear.

**Figure 4.22**

```
welcome - EXEC                                                    _ □ ×
T 12 x 20 ▾
CHECK OUT FOR ROOM   204            AMOUNT DUE:       93.50
                                    AGREED PAY METHOD: MS    CREDIT:   500.00
LAST NAME:  COLM
                                    09/27      1   ROOM                  85.00
TITLE: MS       FIRST: DOTTIE       09/27          TAX                    8.50

***   GUEST ADDRESS    ***
1001 HYPERTEXT WAY
SAN JOSE, CA

    TELE#: 555-0101

** ADDITIONAL ADDRESS **




COMMENTS:
CASHIER I.D.:
ACTUAL PAYMENT METHOD: MS
CR CARD / CL#:5468 1001 1000 1101

HIST?   #1 0000 #2 0000 #3 0000     ROOM VACATE TIME:   :   (SKIP IF NOW)
PRESS "PgUp" TO POST
                                                    0360101-000000
```

**Figure 4.23**

Next press the Enter key to display the screen shown in Figure 4.23, which displays the folio and statement information for Ms. Colm.

Notice that the details of the current folio statement appear in the top right-hand area of the screen and that the system is prompting for the CASHIER ID; therefore, enter your CASHIER ID, leaving the ACTUAL PAYMENT METHOD as MS. Press Enter to skip through the remaining fields and to complete the check-out process. To verify that the room is empty, select option 3, from the main screen and enter room 204; the screen in Figure 4.24 will appear.

```
welcome - EXEC                                                    _ □ ×
T 12 x 20 ▾
|C 1   SCREEN 01          INNSTAR / SULLKLIN INN        09/28/00 00:06

         REGISTRATION      SHIFT =          CASHIER

      1 = CHECK IN W/RESV           6 = POST TO FOLIO
      2 = WALK IN GUEST             7 = CHECK OUT
      3 = DISPLAY/CHANGE            E-CHECK IN
      4 = ROOM CHANGE      SHOW FOLIO     RINT STATEMENT
      5 = ROOM ALLOCATIO            HIFT REPORT
      A = ARRIVALS       ROOM NUMBER: 204  OSTINGS SCAN

           STATUS                            OTHER

      B = ROOM AVAILABILITY        R = RESERVATIONS
      D = DEPARTURES               T = TELEPHONE
      K = SHOW RACK (O, V)         H = HOUSEKEEPING
      S = ROOM STATUS SCAN         M = MAINTENANCE
      X = SET ROOM STATUS          U = RESTAURANTS
      Y = SET ROOM CONDITION       F = FUNCTIONS/BANQUET
      Z = SHOW HOUSE STATUS        J = CITY LEDGER
      N = FRONT DESK REPORTS       E = TRAVEL AGENT
      Q = OTHER                    G = GUEST HISTORY
      * = HELP    L = LOG OFF      W = WORD PROCESSING
*** ROOM IS VACANT              3
                                                    0240101-000000
```

**Figure 4.24**

The words "ROOM IS VACANT" appear at the bottom left of the screen. This signals that the check-out is complete; the printed folio for Ms. Colm will be at your printer. The check-out process will change the status of the room in Innstar to VACANT; after the NIGHT AUDIT has been run, the HOUSEKEEPING STATUS will read as DIRTY.

## Cashier End-of-Shift Reporting

At the end of each shift, the front-office cashier is responsible for preparing a report that summarizes the accounting work completed during the shift. Innstar has a function that captures the work of the cashier and presents the report in a very organized format so that the screen information can be cross-checked with the actual printed documentation of each transaction. In our current example, the only transaction completed is the check-out of room 204. Let's prepare the SHIFT REPORT by selecting option C from the main screen (Figure 4.25).

From this screen you will process the CASHIER SHIFT REPORT. *Do not* enter any data at this time, however, as you can only run this report once; therefore, use these instructions only when you are doing your homework at the end of this chapter.

Enter 50000 (to represent $500.00) in the DRAWER OPENING BALANCE field to denote that the cashier started the shift with a bank of $500.00 cash. Press Enter to skip the PRINTER NUMBER (since, for now, we will look at this report only on the screen). Next press Page Down to skip the SHIFT and CASHIER(S) fields; this will give us all the transactions for all shifts and cashiers.

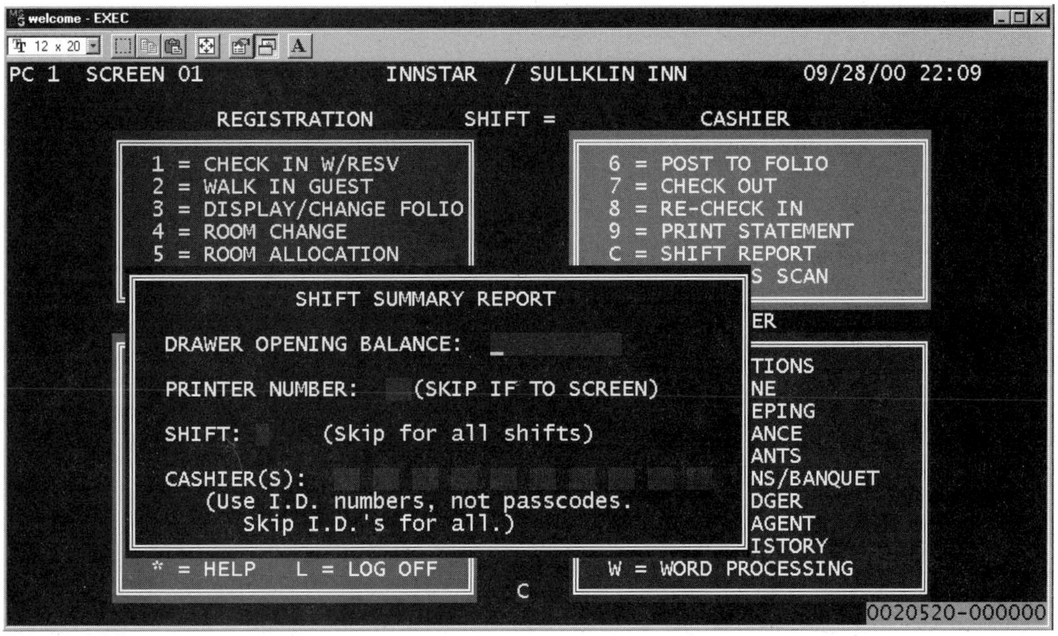

**Figure 4.25**

```
welcome - EXEC                                                      _□X
T 12 x 20 ▾  ▢▢▢ ▢ ▢▢ A
SULLKLIN INN           SHIFT REPORT  09/28/00  00:13   CASHIERS = ALL
SHIFT = ALL            FRONT DESK       DEPOSITS*    CITY LEDGER*      TOTALS
OPENING BALANCE =        500.00CR                                   500.00CR
  + CASH       =         225.00CR           .00           .00       225.00CR
  + CHECK      =          50.00CR        220.00CR          .00       270.00CR
  - PAID OUT   =            .00                                         .00
  - REFUND     =            .00                                         .00
  - PETTY CASH =            .00                                         .00
CLOSING BALANCE =        775.00CR        220.00CR          .00       995.00CR
CREDIT CARD RECEIPTS:
          CK =            50.00CR        220.00CR          .00       270.00CR
          AX =           119.00CR           .00           .00       119.00CR
          VI =             .00              .00           .00          .00
          MS =           209.75CR           .00           .00       209.75CR
          DS =             .00              .00           .00          .00
          DB =             .00              .00           .00          .00
          XF =             .00              .00           .00          .00

TRANSFERS           .00           .00           .00    * IN BALANCE *



**DEPOSITS & C/L NOT TOTALED BY SHIFT** (TYPE "D" FOR DETAILS, "P" TO PRINT)
                                                      0601801-000000
```

**Figure 4.26**

For individual work, using the CASHIER function can be more specific; in our example, it does not matter, since only one cashier is working. As you press page down, the screen in Figure 4.26 will appear.

Notice the CASH and CHECK rows reflect the funds collected during the day. The cash CLOSING BALANCE would be impacted by typical cash transactions, such as CASH PAYMENTS, PAID OUTS, and CHECKS. The CLOSING BALANCE is the amount of cash that should not be present in the cashier's cash drawer. Normally the amount of the BANK (in this case $500.00) would be removed prior to making the bank deposit for the balance. Differences in the CLOSING BALANCE and the actual cash would signify cashier overage or shortage.

The next section of the CASHIER REPORT deals with CREDIT CARD RECEIPTS, where we can balance the work by PAYMENT METHOD to match the TOTALS in this report by CREDIT CARD TYPE. As the shift progresses, the cashier would manually sort the work by METHOD OF PAYMENT and then reconcile that total with this report. In most hotels, the cashier is responsible for running this report, reconciling the work with the screen report, then printing the report to be submitted with the shift's work. Accuracy is vital, since impacts on folios and other payments are the main manner in which the hotel collects revenue.

## Chapter 4 Exercises

Name _____ Date _____

1) Mr. Graw in room 201 has made three local calls. Each local call costs $.50.  The reference numbers for these calls are 01, 02, and 03. The reference comment is "local."   Explain how you posted these calls to the folio.

   _____

   _____

   _____

   _____

2) List the type of charges that may be used to post to rooms in this program.

   _____

   _____

   _____

   _____

3) List the type of credits that may be used to post to rooms in this program.

   _____

   _____

   _____

   _____

   _____

4) Mr. Levy would like to pay cash to cover the cost of his call to London. He is in room 103.  Review the statement and locate the call to London in the record.  Tell Mr. Levy the cost of that call.  Mr. Levy pays cash for the phone call.  Post the cash payment using the reference number "01" and the comment "pd cash."
   How much was the call to London?_____
   Explain the steps you took to post the cash to Mr. Levy's room.

   _____

   _____

   _____

   _____

   _____

5) Your friend and fellow desk clerk has made a mistake and needs your help to correct the error. It seems that he posted the same transaction twice. He tells you that he posted two movie charges to Ms. Lauren William's room, number 202. He goes on to say that she should only be charged for one movie. Make the appropriate changes to Ms. William's folio. Explain to your friend how you made the correction so that he will know how to correct this type of problem in the future.

_____

_____

_____

_____

_____

6) Oops! While posting long-distance telephone calls you accidentally posted a call to Paris, France, to the wrong room number. Mr. Levy in room 103 actually placed the call but you just posted it to room 108. In order to correct this posting error you need to transfer this transaction to the correct room. Correct the posting error and explain the steps you took to transfer this transaction to the proper room number.

_____

_____

_____

_____

_____

7) Ms. Williams in room 202 would like to check out. Please check her out and explain the steps you took to ensure a smooth and professionally handled departure. Describe the check-out process.

_____

_____

_____

_____

_____

8) Run the end-of-shift report.  Your beginning bank was $500.00, and you work on shift number 1. Write the amounts on your shift report below.

| | |
|---|---|
| Opening balance | $_____ |
| Cash | $_____ |
| Check | $_____ |
| Any credit card receipts | $_____ |
| Closing balance | $_____ |

# CHAPTER 5
# GUEST SERVICES

## Key Learning Concepts in Chapter 5
Housekeeping
- Room Status
- Room Condition

Maintenance
- Work Orders

Telephone
- Message Services
- Guest Search

## Housekeeping

Housekeeping involves a very important series of functions in any lodging property, because it directly impacts the quality of the guest experience in the room. Cleanliness always ranks high on the list of issues that are important to guests and is one of the major reasons that they become or don't become repeat customers.

While the list of housekeeping options in a typical PMS varies, all contain the major functions, which can be demonstrated very well in Innstar. Let's start by going to the HOUSEKEEPING menu in Innstar, by selecting H, for HOUSEKEEPING (Figure 5.1).

```
welcome - EXEC                                                    _ □ ×
T 12 x 20                      A
PC 1   SCREEN 01        INNSTAR  / SULLKLIN INN      09/28/00 21:52

                            HOUSEKEEPING

                1 = SET STAT / COND
                2 = SET ROOM CONDITION
                3 = SET ROOM STATUS
                4 = DISCREPANCIES
                K = SHOW RACK (O, V)
                S = ROOM STATUS SCAN
                Z = SHOW HOUSE STATUS
                B = DAILY SUMMARY
                M = MAINTENANCE
                C = CRIBS
                R = ROLLAWAY BEDS
                D = DEPARTURES
                F = LOST & FOUND
                U = UNEXPECTED DEPARTURE
                H = HSKP ROOMS REPORT
                + = CALCULATOR
                W = WORD PROCESSING
                * = HELP   L = LOG OFF

                          —
                                              0021101-000000
```

**Figure 5.1**

Two of the primary PMS functions that Innstar manages are ROOM STATUS and ROOM CONDITION. ROOM STATUS in Innstar refers to the occupancy status of the room, normally denoted either by O, for occupied, or V, for vacant" in the system. Typically, the Innstar PMS will update the room status automatically using the registration and check-out process. As a guest is registered, the system changes ROOM STATUS from V to O, denoting that the room is occupied. At check-out, the system will again automatically update the status in reverse, from O to V denoting that the room has been vacated. It is also possible to manually change the ROOM STATUS, by selecting option 1, SET STAT/COND. This will display a screen that requests a ROOM NUMBER; enter "101," as shown in Figure 5.2.

The screen that appears gives you the options to change the ROOM STATUS from V, VACANT to O, OCCUPIED. Enter "O" as shown in Figure 5.3.

```
welcome - EXEC                                                          _ □ ×
T 12 x 20 ▾  □ ▣ ▣ ▣ ▣ ▣ A
PC 1  SCREEN 01              INNSTAR  / SULLKLIN INN       09/28/00 22:01

CHANGE ROOM STATUS / CONDITION              ┌─────────────────────────────┐
                                            │ VALID STATUS & CONDITION    │
ROOM: 101                                   │                             │
                                            │ V = VACANT     D = DIRTY    │
                                            │ O = OCCUPIED   C = CLEAN    │
                                            │                I = INSPECTED│
                                            └─────────────────────────────┘
```

**Figure 5.2**

```
welcome - EXEC                                                          _ □ ×
T 12 x 20 ▾  □ ▣ ▣ ▣ ▣ ▣ A
PC 1  SCREEN 01              INNSTAR  / SULLKLIN INN       09/28/00 22:01

CHANGE ROOM STATUS / CONDITION              ┌─────────────────────────────┐
                                            │ VALID STATUS & CONDITION    │
ROOM:  101  DD    V    I                    │                             │
                                            │ V = VACANT     D = DIRTY    │
STATUS: O CONDITION: _                      │ O = OCCUPIED   C = CLEAN    │
                                            │                I = INSPECTED│
                                            └─────────────────────────────┘



                                                        0030901-000000
```

**Figure 5.3**

Next enter "I" in the CONDITION FIELD; this will display the screen shown in Figure 5.4.

The system will not, however, allow you to change the ROOM STATUS in this manner, and that is good management practice: you must RE-CHECK ROOM, since it cannot be occupied without a proper REGISTRATION.

The next housekeeping function deals with the condition of the room. In Innstar there are three basic ROOM CONDITION status options: I for INSPECTED (meaning the room is fully ready for sale and has been re-checked by a supervisor), C for CLEAN (meaning the room has been cleaned by the room attendant and is now ready for occupancy or inspection, depending on the internal practices of the property), and D for DIRTY (meaning the room has been occupied and needs to be cleaned by a room attendant before it can be reused or occupied for another day or by another guest).

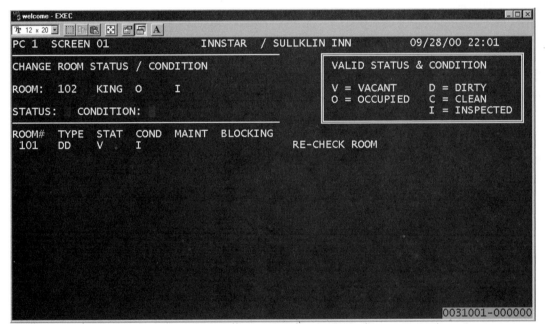

**Figure 5.4**

Normally, updating ROOM CONDITION is started by the NIGHT AUDIT process, where rooms that are shown as OCCUPIED are automatically changed from I, INPSECTED, to D, DIRTY, when the NIGHT AUDIT functions are run. Reports are produced for the housekeeping supervisors to indicate which rooms are D, DIRTY, so that room attendants can be scheduled to clean them. Once the room attendant has cleaned the room, there are several ways to update ROOM CONDITION in Innstar. The first and most common is to use a telephone interface that allows the room attendant to dial into the system to change the status from the guest room phone. This is an excellent process to use, since it rapidly updates the CONDITION of the room so that it is available for sale as soon as the INSPECTION process is done. If the property uses an INSPECTION process, the housekeeping supervisor can also update ROOM CONDITION from C, CLEAN, to I, INSPECTED using the same phone interface connection. If the telephone interface is not installed, or cannot be used, ROOM CONDITION can be updated manually. To do this, from the HOUSEKEEPING screen, select option 2, SET ROOM CONDITION.I In this case, enter room 101 and the screen shown in Figure 5.5 will appear.

```
welcome - EXEC                                                        _ □ ×
 T 12 x 20 ▾   ▭ ▤ ▣ ▣ ▣ ▣ A
PC 1  SCREEN 01              INNSTAR  / SULLKLIN INN        09/28/00 22:08

CHANGE ROOM CONDITION                           ┌─────────────────────────┐
                                                │ VALID ROOM CONDITIONS   │
ROOM: 101                                       │                         │
                                                │   D = DIRTY             │
ENTER CONDITION:      (R = CHANGE ROOM #)        │   C = CLEAN             │
                                                │   I = INSPECTED         │
                                                │   P = PICK UP           │
                                                └─────────────────────────┘



                                                             0030201-000000
```

**Figure 5.5**

```
welcome - EXEC                                                    _ □ ×
 ⊤ 12 x 20 ▾  □ ⊡ ⓖ ⊡ ⓖ ⓖ A
PC 1  SCREEN 01              INNSTAR  / SULLKLIN INN      09/28/00 22:08

CHANGE ROOM CONDITION                    ┌──────────────────────────┐
                                         │ VALID ROOM CONDITIONS    │
ROOM:  102   KING  O     I               │                          │
                                         │   D = DIRTY              │
ENTER CONDITION:  C   (R = CHANGE ROOM #)│   C = CLEAN              │
                                         │   I = INSPECTED          │
─────────────────────────────────────── │   P = PICK UP            │
ROOM#  TYPE  STAT  COND  MAINT  BLOCKING └──────────────────────────┘
 101   DD    V     C




                                                      0030401-000000
```

**Figure 5.6**

Figure 5.6 shows that room 101 currently is listed as having the ROOM CONDITION status of I, INSPECTED. Enter C to change the status to CLEAN. After you enter the "c" your screen will change and look like Figure 5.6.

Note that room 101 is now shown as C, CLEAN in the COND field. The system now prompts for a change for the next room in the system, room 102, since normally the person inputting changes will be updating a number of rooms. At this point, however, we will not update any other rooms, so press the Esc key to return to the main menu.

The process for updating ROOM STATUS and ROOM CONDITION varies from PMS to PMS, but the importance of these functions remains the same, as they clearly impact guest service. Ask any guest who has been booked in an occupied or dirty room, and they will give a first-hand opinion of how the property operates!

## Work Orders

Many PMS systems have a module for managing work orders for guest rooms. Proper functioning of all systems in the guest rooms is vital to maintaining the quality of the property and its reputation. The WORK ORDER module of Innstar allows the staff to manage requests related to conditions in the room from either the guests or staff, and to track the work order to completion. The WORK ORDER module can be accessed from the H, HOUSEKEEPING, screen by selecting M for MAINTENANCE; the screen in Figure 5.7 will appear.

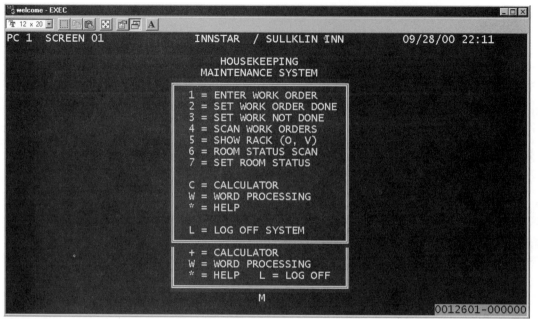

**Figure 5.7**

This list of options allows us to enter, update, and scan work orders that relate to guest rooms. To enter a WORK ORDER, select option 1, ENTER WORK ORDER (Figure 5.8).

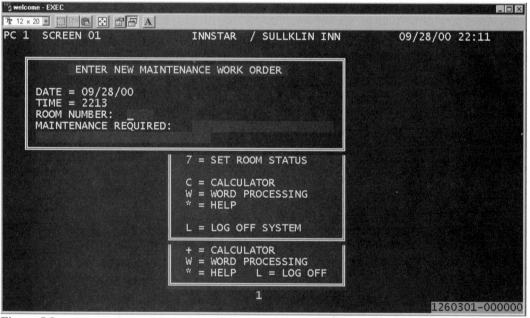

**Figure 5.8**

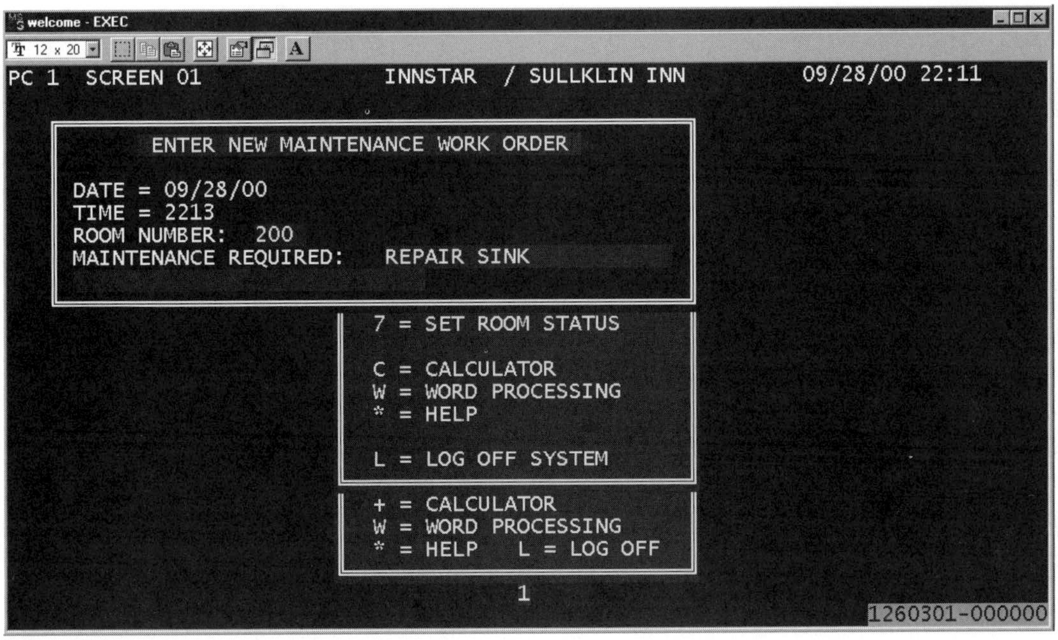

**Figure 5.9**

Enter "200" for the ROOM NUMBER, and type in "REPAIR SINK" in the MAINTENANCE REQUIRED field, as shown in Figure 5.9. Next, press Enter twice to see the screen shown in Figure 5.10.

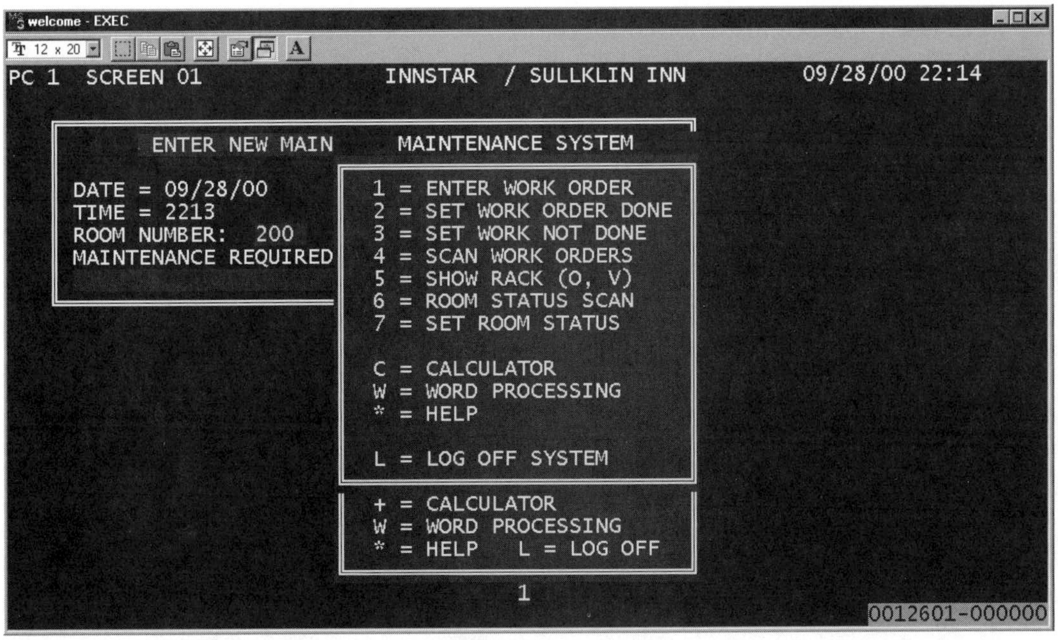

**Figure 5.10**

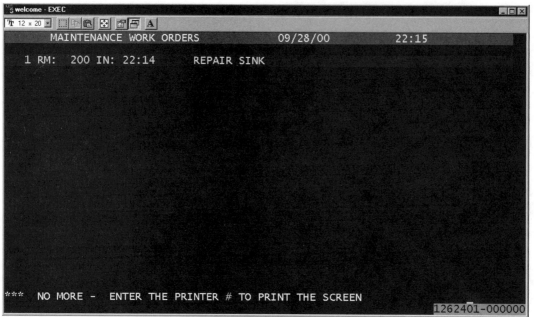

**Figure 5.11**

To scan open WORK ORDERS, first select 4 for SCAN WORK ORDERS, then A for all
WORK ORDERS; the screen in Figure 5.11 will appear. Note that this is WORK ORDER 1;
Innstar numbers the WORK ORDERS as they are entered, for follow-up.

This shows the work order that we just entered for room 200. Now press the Esc key to return the
main menu. Again select H for HOUSEKEEPING, then M for MAINTENANCE; next select
option 2, for SET WORK ORDER DONE, then enter 1, for FINISHED WORK ORDER 1
(Figure 5.12).

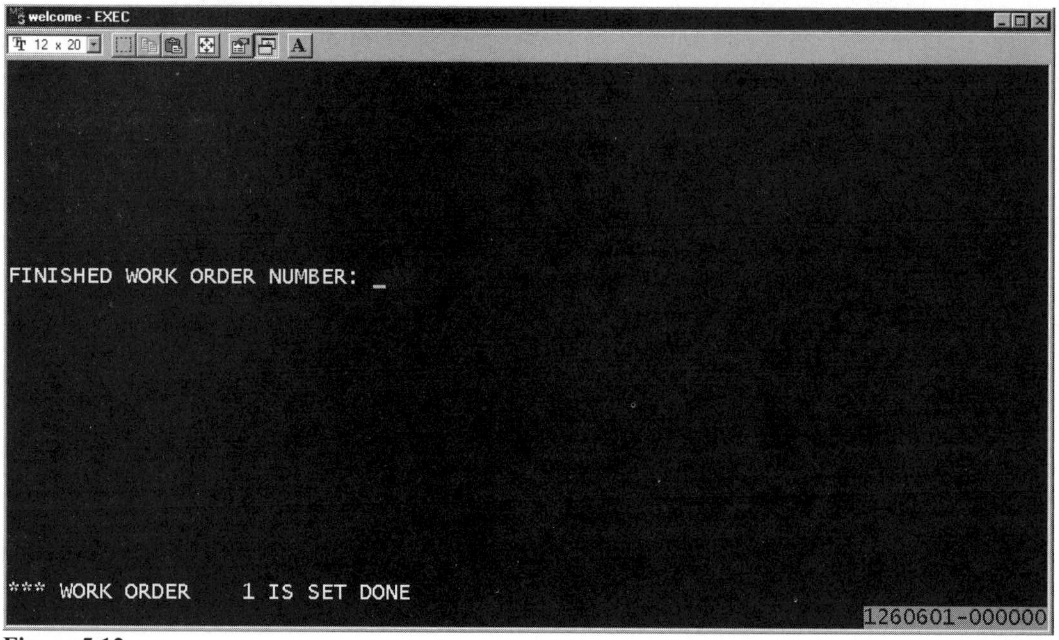

**Figure 5.12**

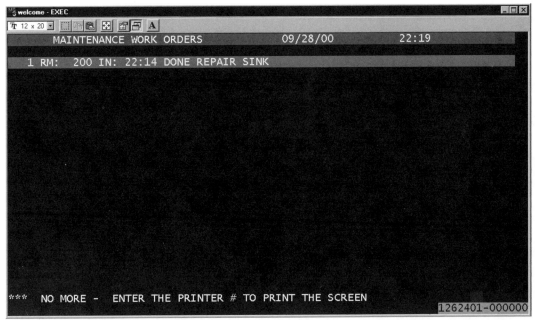

**Figure 5.13**

Now let's return one more time to HOUSEKEEPING screen by selecting H, then M for MAINTENACE; select 4 again to SCAN WORK ORDERS, and the screen that appears next will show the time and date that WORK ORDER 1 was completed (Figure 5.13).

Having up-to-date information available on all areas of the property is an important part of the follow-up process for both the guests and staff. From any screen with access to the WORK ORDER process, staff can inform a guest of the date and time that the work order was completed.  Guests appreciate prompt repair and follow-up to requests for room repairs.

## Telephone Services

Access to guests by telephone is a key part of the communications process at any property. Innstar has a standard set of TELEPHONE service functions that are accessible from the main screen by selecting T for TELEPHONE (Figure 5.14).

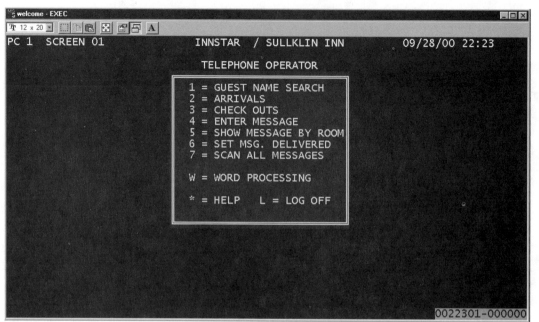

**Figure 5.14**

When an outside person calls the property to be connected with a guest, the most common option used is 1, for GUEST NAME SEARCH; this allows an alphabetic search of the guests who are currently registered. The screen appears as in Figure 5.15.

**Figure 5.15**

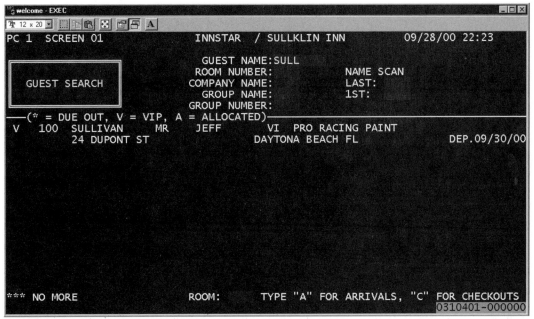

**Figure 5.16**

This screen allows for several ways to find the guest. For this example, type "SULL" as the GUEST NAME; press the Page Down key to skip the other search options. The screen in Figure 5.16 will appear.

If the guest cannot be found, it usually indicates one of three things: the name in incorrect, the guest has not checked in yet, or the guest has already checked out. Return to the TELEPHONE screen by selecting T (refer back to Figure 5.14); you can see, there are options for looking at ARRIVALS (OPTION 2) and CHECK-OUTS (OPTION 3). You would use these options as needed to determine the current status of the guest for phone services.

From that same TELEPHONE screen, let's now look at the MESSAGE services that are available in Innstar. Many properties have a VOICE MAIL service, which functions much like a home or office system; still, there are callers who prefer to leave a message for a guest that will be delivered personally by a member of the staff of the property. To do this, normally the guest is notified via a message light on the guest room phone or by physical delivery of the message to the guest room. To take a MESSAGE in Innstar, select 4 for ENTER MESSAGE to access the screen shown in Figure 5.17.

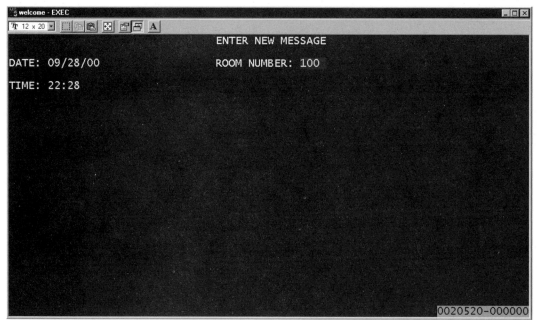

**Figure 5.17**

```
welcome - EXEC                                                    _ □ ×
T 12 x 20 ▼  □▣▣ ▣ ▣▣ A
                      FOLIOS IN ROOM #:   100


               1 = SULLIVAN      JEFF

               2 =

               3 =

               4 =

               5 =
               °
               6 =




          CHOOSE GUEST BY ENTERING FOLIO #:
                                              0371001-000000
```

**Figure 5.18**

Enter "100" in the ROOM NUMBER field, and the screen in Figure 5.18 will appear. As you can see, this allows for messages to be delivered to multiple guests in the room and for the selection of the proper message.

Select 1, for SULLIVAN; on the next screen, enter "01" for ID and "CALL OFFICE AT 999-0909," as shown in Figure 5.19.

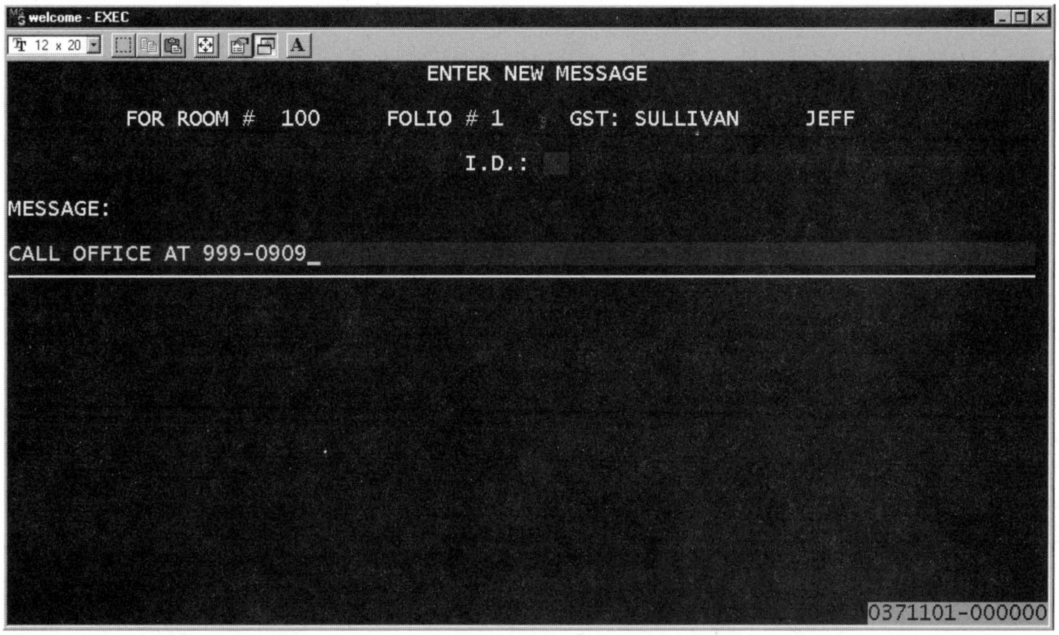

```
welcome - EXEC                                                    _ □ ×
T 12 x 20 ▼ □ ⬚ ⬚ ⬚ ⬚ ⬚ A
                          ENTER NEW MESSAGE
            FOR ROOM #  100      FOLIO # 1    GST: SULLIVAN      JEFF
                              I.D.:  ▪
MESSAGE:
CALL OFFICE AT 999-0909_
_____




                                                        0371101-000000
```

**Figure 5.19**

After you complete entry of the message, press the Enter key to return to the main menu screen.
Select T, TELEPHONE, then 7 for SCAN ALL MESSAGES; the screen in Figure 5.20 will
appear.

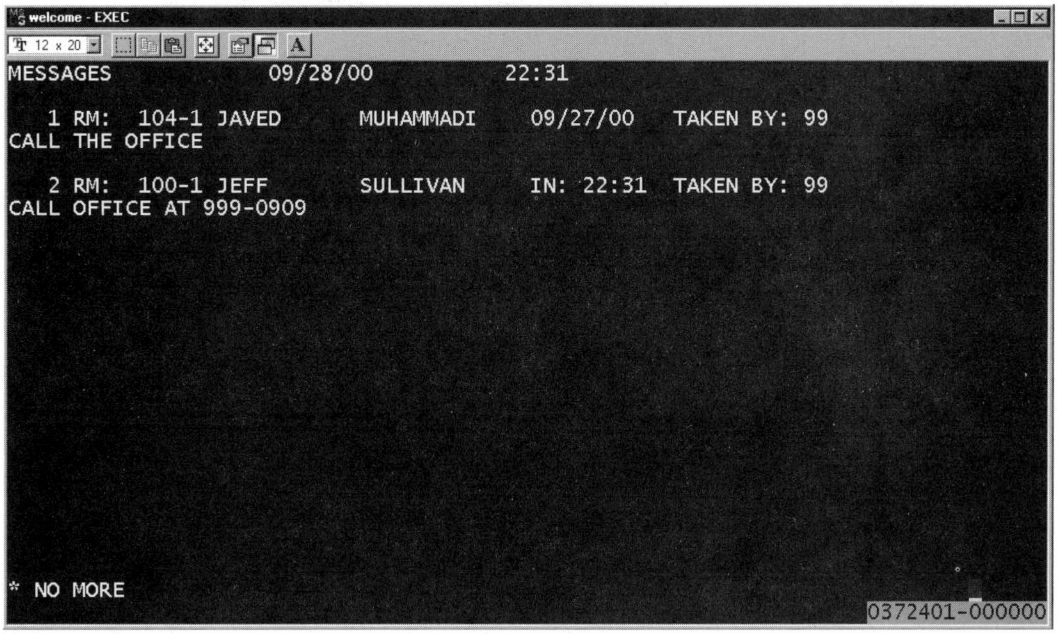

```
welcome - EXEC                                                    _ □ ×
T 12 x 20 ▼ □ ⬚ ⬚ ⬚ ⬚ ⬚ A
MESSAGES              09/28/00          22:31

    1 RM:  104-1 JAVED      MUHAMMADI    09/27/00   TAKEN BY: 99
CALL THE OFFICE

    2 RM:  100-1 JEFF       SULLIVAN     IN: 22:31  TAKEN BY: 99
CALL OFFICE AT 999-0909









* NO MORE
                                                        0372401-000000
```

**Figure 5.20**

This screen shows the message that we just entered for room 100, noting the time and the ID of the staff person who took the message. Now select option 6, SET MSG. DELIVERED; then enter room "100," FOLIO "1," and ID "01." The screen shown in Figure 5.21 will appear indicating that the message has been delivered.

Guests place a high value on efficient and timely message delivery, so this function, too, is key to providing high-quality guest service. The Innstar PMS MESSAGES functionality is a simple, yet effective way to track receipt and delivery of guest messages.

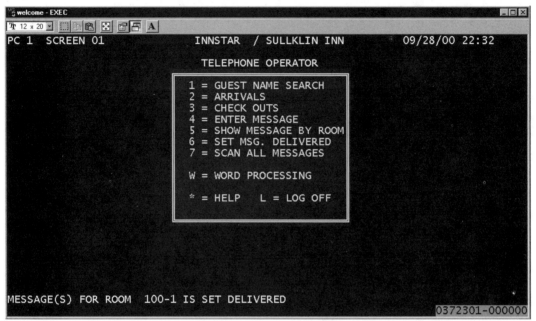

**Figure 5.21**

## Chapter 5 Exercises

Name _____   Date _____

1) What is the difference between the room condition and the room status? Give examples of each.

_____

_____

_____

_____

_____

2) Explain the normal process for changing room status from INSPECTED to DIRTY for occupied rooms. How and when does the Innstar system handle this procedure?

_____

_____

_____

_____

_____

3) View the room rack by entering K. How many rooms are vacant and how many rooms are occupied?
   Number of vacant rooms _____
   Number of occupied rooms _____
   List the room numbers for each occupied room.

_____

   List the room numbers for each dirty room.

_____

4) You receive a report from the executive housekeeper. Based on that report you make the following changes in the PMS system.

   Change the status of all DIRTY rooms to reflect that housekeeping has cleaned and inspected them.

5) View the room rack again by entering K.
   Number of vacant rooms _____
   Number of occupied rooms _____

List the room numbers for each occupied room.

_____

List the room numbers for each dirty room.

_____

6) Check the PMS system for all outstanding work orders. Record each room number and corresponding maintenance problem in your workbook.

_____

_____

7) Mr. Kline in room 201 calls because the remote control on his television does not work. Create a work order for this maintenance request.

8) Fred Phixit, the head of maintenance, calls the front desk to report that the sink in room 108 has been repaired. Make that change in the PMS system.

9) Check the PMS system for all outstanding work orders. Record each room number and corresponding maintenance problem in your workbook.

_____

_____

10) While at the front desk you receive a phone call for Ms. Chrissy. She is not in the room so you leave a message for her from Serge. The message is to have her call the shop ASAP.

11) Mr. Eubuzzoffsky is not in his room, and the caller would like to leave a message. The call is from his mother and reads, "Please call your mother when you get in."

12) Scan all messages in the PMS system and record the room numbers, guest names, and corresponding messages in the workbook.

_____

_____

_____

_____

_____

13) A man walks up to the front desk and is looking for a guest, Mr. Muhamadi. He explains that Mr. Muhamadi is supposed to meet him in the lobby but is not there. You offer to call the room for the gentleman.
   a) What is Mr. Muhamadi's room number? _____

b)  Explain how you would handle this situation.

_____

_____

_____

_____

_____

# CHAPTER 6

# NIGHT AUDIT

## Key Learning Concepts in Chapter 6
- How to review the purpose of the night audit.
- How to run the night audit using Innstar.
- How to post room and tax.
- How to review key printed reports.
- How to analyze end-of-day reports.

The night audit occurs at the end of the hotel's business day. It is actually an audit of the account receivables from the day. In this workbook, the night audit is reflects all the transactions that occurred on September 28, 2000. When the night audit is completed, the business day ends and the next day begins. In a real hotel, the night audit actually occurs during the graveyard shift, some time between 11:00 P.M. and 7:00 A.M.

During the night audit, many reports are printed and reviewed. The purpose of the night audit is to review the guest and nonguest accounts and ensure that they are correct. Also during the night audit, transactions are verified, room and tax is posted, and accounts are balanced. The night audit functions must be performed at the end of each business day because the date of the system will not change until it is done. Revenue reports are printed when the night audit is run.

The night auditor's job is to verify information and determine whether it is correct. The night auditor also determines whether the clerks entered the correct rates in the folios. In a real hotel, the night auditor would ensure that the check-out charges on the credit card vouchers were correct and that the guests had signed the vouchers. The auditor also checks to see whether the management has approved the discounted rates. He or she would ensure that phone calls and maintenance requests had been posted properly. Then, in a real hotel, the auditor would balance the cash and receipts.

Before starting the night audit, all transactions must be posted. So, for the purpose of this workbook, before running the end-of-day reports, the student should have completed all of the examples and homework assignments in the preceding chapters. Only then may the student proceed with the night audit.

Start at Innstar's main menu and go to OTHER by pressing Q, then N for NIGHT AUDIT. Figure 6.1 shows the screen that asks for a pass code. In a real hotel, a manager's or night auditor's passcode would be assigned. In this workbook, there are no pass codes, so hit the Enter key to bypass the PASS CODE field. This is true for all PASS CODE fields where students are permitted access.

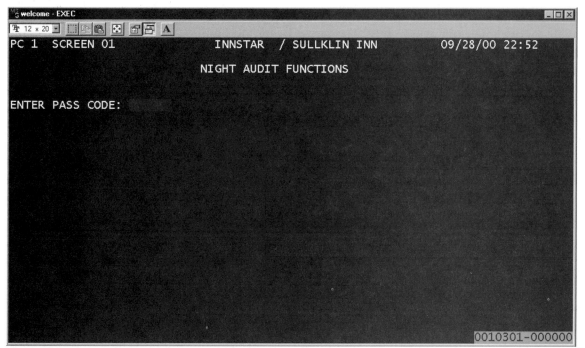

**Figure 6.1**

Innstar allows the night audit to be performed in two ways: one is automated and the other is manual. We will be using the manual method, so enter M for manual (Figure 6.2).

**Figure 6.2**

The main night audit screen shows two boxes. The box on the left lists the main night audit reports that most hotels run every night. The box on the right includes night audit reports that are run before the end of the day and reports that are run after the night audit. We will focus on the reports located on the left side of the screen, as shown in Figure 6.3.

We will be running most, but not all, of the reports on the left side of the screen. Stating at the top, we will run each report. All reports/functions (except for Z, FILE MAINTENANCE) can be performed as many times as you would like.

*Do not run* the Z report until you have posted room and tax and have printed all desired reports. Z is the critical function, as it changes the date on the system and zeroes out all of figures from September 28. There is no turning back once this report is run.

When a report is run, it does not appear on the screen; rather, it is printed. It will print one of two ways, depending upon the configuration of your hardware and software. In most environments, the report will print immediately after you input the command for the report, but in some cases you will need to log out of the system after pressing the command for the report.

If your printer does not print the report, log out of Innstar by returning to the main menu, then press L to log out, and type "QUIT." The report will print after you quit out of the system. After you retrieve the report from the printer, start up the Innstar program and proceed to the next report.

In some cases the local printer settings may need to be changed. If your reports didn't print follow these instructions to change your printer settings. Go to "Control Panel" from the "start" button. Then go to "Printer". Then under "Detail" select "Port Settings". Then remove the "x" from the "Spool MS-DOS" printing jobs. Go back to the Innstar program and continue to run the reports.

Because this is a software simulation and not an actual hotel, we will not run any of the back-up reports. However, this is a very important function in a real hotel.

We will begin with the ROOM RATE REPORT.

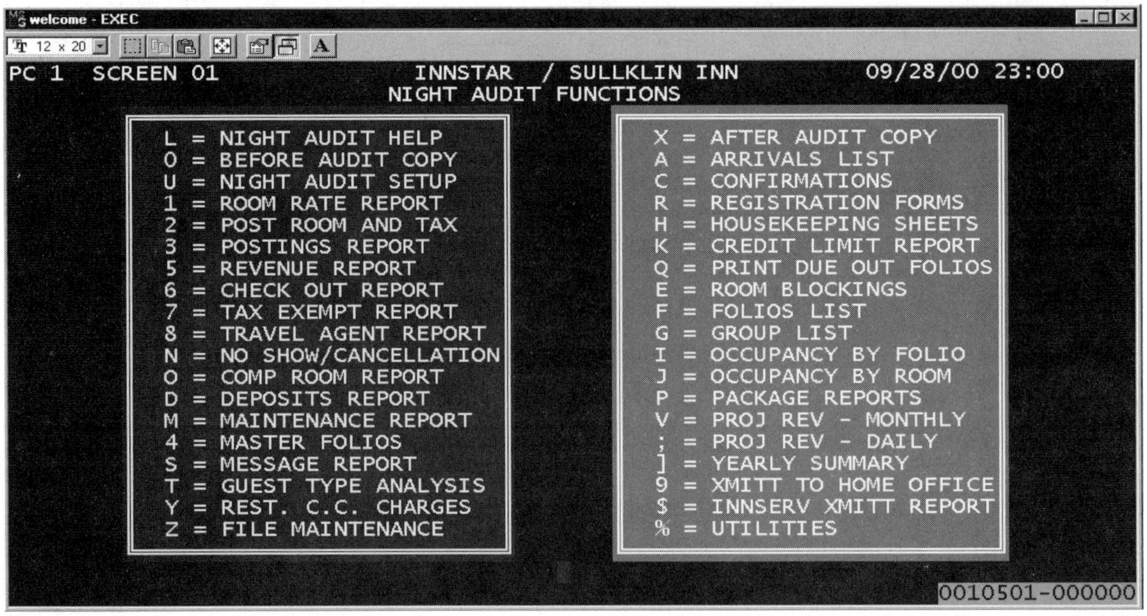

Figure 6.3

**Room Rate Report (1)**

The first report we will print is the ROOM RATE REPORT. Press 1 to get this report. When the screen shown in Figure 6.4 appears, you will be prompted to press any key but the Esc key. Hit the Enter key and print to print the ROOM RATE REPORT. This screen will appear for each report except the Z report. Use the Enter key after each report command to print all the reports. Once you press Enter, a message on the computer will state that the system is "processing" the report. The report will print after that message disappears from the screen. If the report does not print, refer to the printing information at the beginning of this chapter.

Let's review this report by looking at Report 6.1 (located at the end of this chapter). This report is used primarily to review and verify each room rate.

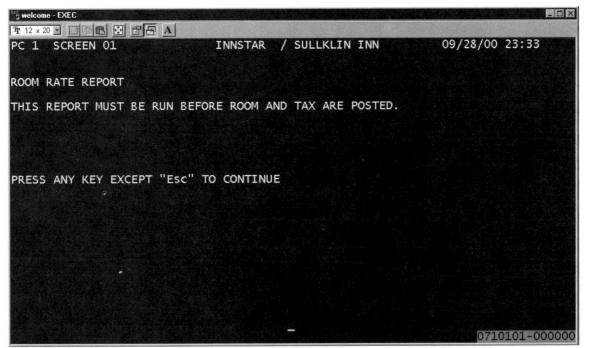

**Figure 6.4**

The ROOM RATE REPORT prints the following: a record of each occupied room, the room rate based on the rack rate, the folio rate and what will be posted today, and the resulting rate variance. It will also print out the guest name, segment, and tariff type of each folio; the guest's company and/or group name; whether the room is tax-exempt, part of a package, along with manual room and tax postings. The night auditor reviews this report to ensure that all rates are accurate and to recover any potentially lost revenue by verifying the discounted rates that have been authorized by management.

At the end of this report, a total variance by tariff type is printed. Information includes the tariff name, the day's total amount of revenue for each tariff type as defined by each rate table, the day's total amount of revenue for each tariff type that is actually in the guest folios, and the resulting variance. It is possible to review the variances of room rates versus rack rates using this information.

If a rate is not correct, go back to folio and change the rate. The procedure to change a rate is to return to the Innstar main menu and enter 3, the room number, and 2. Make the necessary changes and then print the ROOM RATE REPORT again.

### Post Room and Tax (2)

This command posts room and tax to each occupied room. The approximate time that it takes to post room and tax is less than one minute. This function should not be performed before running the ROOM RATE REPORT and checking for rate discrepancies. To run this report, go to the NIGHT AUDIT FUNCTION menu (Figure 6.3) and press 2, then C to continue to post the room and tax. This will result in a printout that contains no information. See Report 6.2 at the end of this chapter.

### Postings Report (3)

To run the POSTINGS REPORT, press 3 from the NIGHT AUDIT FUNCTIONS screen (Figure 6.3), then press Enter to continue. The system should take less than one minute to process this request.

The POSTINGS REPORT reports each posting transaction, grouped by revenue or credit department. It shows the amount, room number, clerk ID, and reference number. This is the same type of report that you would get from a journal tape in a cash register. Report 6.3 located at the end of this chapter shows a copy of the POSTINGS REPORT.

### Revenue Report (5)

To run the REVENUE REPORT, press 5 from the NIGHT AUDIT FUNCTIONS screen (Figure 6.3) and press Enter to continue. The system should take less than one minute to process this request.

The REVENUE REPORT is in a summarized format (the POSTINGS REPORT is the detailed format). When running this manually, this is the "trial balance" report. This report is also automatically printed when the Z, FILE MAINTENANCE, is performed. In a semiautomated system, it is sometimes referred to as the "flash report" or "D-card." A sample REVENUE REPORT is given as Report 6.4 at the end of this chapter.

### Check-out Report (6)

To run the CHECK-OUT REPORT, press 6 from the NIGHT AUDIT FUNCTIONS screen (Figure 6.3), then press Enter to continue. The system should take less than one minute to process this request.

During the day, when a guest checks out, the hotel typically maintains a copy of that guest's check-out folio. In addition to that copy, or instead of it depending on your preference, this report prints a summarized copy of each folio that was checked out today. Information on all the guests who have checked out is found on Report 6.5 located at the end of this chapter.

For the purposes of this workbook, we will not be printing the TAX-EXEMPT and TRAVEL AGENT report. The next report that we will perform is the NO SHOW/CANCELLATION report.

### No-Show and Cancellation Report (N)

To run the NO-SHOW/CANCELLATION REPORT, press N from the NIGHT AUDIT FUNCTIONS screen (Figure 6.3) and press Enter to continue. The system should take less than one minute to process this request.

The NO SHOW/CANCELLATION REPORT shows all unclaimed reservations that were due in today. Most hotels charge individuals with a guaranteed reservation the cost of the first night's room rate plus tax. This is typically done by checking in the no-show and then checking out the no-show prior to completing the night audit. This report also prints reservations that were cancelled today. Report 6.6 at the end of this chapter displays the no-shows and cancelled reservations.

### Comp Rooms Report (0)

To run the COMP ROOMS REPORT, press O from the NIGHT AUDIT FUNCTIONS screen (Figure 6.3) and press Enter to continue. This report shows all the rooms that have not been charged room rate. Report 6.7 at the end of this chapter) displays the comped rooms for this property.

### Deposits Report (D-T, D-A, and D-O)

To run the DEPOSITS REPORT, press D from the NIGHT AUDIT FUNCTIONS screen (Figure 6.3) and then T to continue. The system should take less than one minute to process this request.

Option T prints all deposits posted to reservations for today and shows net changes to the deposit ledger, which resulted from cancelled or refunded deposits.

To run the next DEPOSITS REPORT, press A from the DEPOSITS REPORT menu. Option A prints all deposits that have been received (posted to the reservation) but have not yet been applied—that is, all deposits on file. After pressing A, run the detail report by arrival date.

To run the last DEPOSITS REPORT, press O from the DEPOSITS REPORT menu. Option O prints all reservations in which a deposit was requested by a certain date but has not yet been received—that is, overdue deposits.

A sample DEPOSITS REPORT is shown as Report 6.8 at the end of this chapter.

### Maintenance Report (M)
To run the MAINTENANCE REPORT, press M from the NIGHT AUDIT FUNCTIONS screen (Figure 6.3) and Enter to continue. This report shows both the maintenance work orders that are

outstanding and those that were completed today. Report 6.9 (located at the end of this chapter) shows the work orders for this property.

Though it would be run in a real hotel property, for the purposes of this workbook, we will skip the MASTER FOLIOS REPORT. The next report we will print, then, is the MESSAGE REPORT.

### Message Reports (S)

To run the MESSAGE REPORT, press S from the NIGHT AUDIT FUNCTIONS screen (Figure 6.3) and then Enter to continue.

This report displays all guest messages that were entered into system through function T-4. Those that have not yet been delivered print out on separate pages (so you can deliver them if you want), as well as in report format. The system also prints a report for all messages that have been delivered. Report 6.10 (located at the end of this chapter) displays the message-related reports.

### File Maintenance (Z)

As noted at the beginning of this chapter, the FILE MAINTENANCE REPORT is perhaps the second most important function of the night audit after posting room and tax.  It should be run after all the other reports have been run. In an actual hotel, this report is run after all the revenue and credit departments in the hotel have been balanced, all guests have been checked in, and all charges have been posted to the folios.

Referred to as the "Z-out," running this report essentially ends the current business day and begins the next. It sets the status of all of the occupied rooms in the computer to the D, DIRTY. This takes less than two minutes for the system to perform.

Unlike the other night audit reports, which may be run more than once, the Z, FILE MAINTENANCE REPORT, may be run only once. To do so, press Z from the NIGHT AUDIT FUNCTIONS screen (Figure 6.3) and then G to continue (Figure 6.5).

To complete the night audit and change the date to the next day, you need to run the Z report again.  So press G again and the next screen will appear (Figure 6.6). Now type in the words "RUN AGAIN." In a real hotel, this would change today's date to the next, but because this is a simulation package, the date will not change.

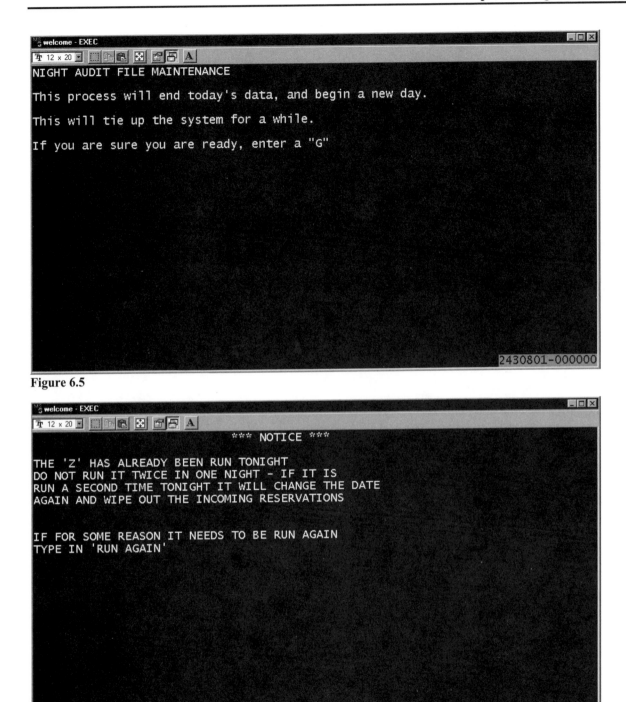

**Figure 6.5**

**Figure 6.6**

The FILE MAINTENANCE REPORT comprises several other reports. First is a REVENUE SUMMARY REPORT. This report is the guest ledger that provides management with separate debit and credit posting totals for the day. A summary of the occupancy and average room rate is given for today, month to date, and year to date.

The ACCOUNTS RECEIVABLE POSTING REPORT lists the account-receivable transfers for the day. This report is followed by the CITY LEDGER REPORT, which is formatted in the same manner as the guest ledger. The city ledger has separate debit and credit posting totals for the day.

The last part of the Z report is the ADVANCED DEPOSITS REPORT. This shows an opening balance, followed by deposits added and subtracted (returned, no-showed, or applied) to give you a new advanced deposit system net.

The final report is the NET OUTSTANDING BALANCE REPORT. It shows the total for advanced deposit activity for the day and the guest ledger balance. This gives you a net outstanding balance for both ledgers.

A sample Z report is found in Report 6.11 at the end of this chapter. Once you have run the Z report, as far as the system is concerned, the day has ended and a new day begins. Your reports will be similar to the ones found in this workbook. Take a few moments and compare them. Note where there are differences. When doing the exercises at the end of this chapter, either use the set of reports from Report 6.1 to 6.11 at the end of this chapter or use your set of reports.

## Chapter 6 Exercises

Name _____ Date _____

1) What is the purpose of the night audit?

_____

_____

_____

_____

_____

_____

_____

_____

2) There are two critical parts of the night audit. What are they and why are they important?

_____

_____

_____

_____

_____

_____

_____

_____

_____

3) Which rooms show a variance in the ROOM RATE REPORT? Provide the room number(s), guest name(s), and amount of the variance(s).

_____

_____

_____

_____

4) Review the POSTINGS REPORT (also called the TRANSACTIONS REPORT).

a) Which guest made the most long-distance phone calls?

_____

b) What corrections were made and to which room numbers?

_____

5) Based on the information found on the guest ledger:

a) What are the total debits for today?

_____

b)  What are the total credits for today?

_____

6)  List the guest names for the check-outs and no-shows for today.

_____

_____

_____

_____

7)  Are there any outstanding maintenance orders?  If so, list them here.

_____

_____

_____

8)  What is the occupancy percentage for today?_____

9)  What is the average daily rate for today?_____

10) In your opinion, how well did the property do today?  How would you describe the day in terms of amount of business and revenue?

_____

_____

_____

_____

_____

_____

_____

_____

## Report 6.1

```
SULLKLIN INN          ROOM RATE REPORT 09/28/00(DOS DATE=01/06) 22:04  PAGE 01


             ROOM    FOLIO  BY  APP
ROOM  TYPE   RATE    RATE   ID  ID  REASON ADL CHILD  TODAY    VARIANCE


100  KING           85.00  99  00  00    01  00     85.00
     JEFF    SULLIVAN    WALK SPEC SPEC PRO RACING  PA          4567 7766 2424 4232
     TOTAL  100.00  85.00               01  00     85.00     15.00--


102  KING          100.00  01  00  00    01  00    100.00
     JORGE   ESTRADA     TRAN STND RACK THREE STAR TRU          3456 2445 3456 2222
     TOTAL  100.00 100.00               01  00    100.00       .00


103  KING          110.00  99  00  00    02  01    110.00
     ELI     LEVY        TRAN STND RACK                         3244 1800 0018 5762
     TOTAL  100.00 110.00               02  01    110.00     10.00


104  DD            85.00  99  00  00    01  00     85.00
     JAVED   MUHAMMADI   TRAN STND RACK                         6778 1001 1110 3456
     TOTAL   85.00  85.00               01  00     85.00       .00


106  DD           100.00  01  00  00    01  00    100.00
     YUKI    TANAKA      TRAN STND RACK                         3700 0125 5552 8040
     TOTAL   85.00 100.00               01  00    100.00     15.00


107  KING         100.00  01  00  00    01  00    100.00
     NELSON  THOMAS      TRAN STND RACK                         
     TOTAL  100.00 100.00               01  00    100.00       .00


108  KING         100.00  99  00  00    01  00    100.00
     HAYWOOD EUBUZZOFFSKY TRAN STND RACK                        3755 2222 2221 2224
     TOTAL  100.00 100.00               01  00    100.00      .00


110  DD            85.00  99  00  00    01  00     85.00
     PIERRE  KLINE       TRAN STND RACK ALLIED MARKETI          5670 0202 3451 5435 6546
     TOTAL   85.00  85.00               01  00     85.00      .00


200  DD            85.00  01  00  00    01  00     85.00
     JOHN    ADAMS       TRAN STND RACK                         5443 3445 5411 1111
     TOTAL   85.00  85.00               01  00     85.00      .00


201  KING          85.00  99  00  00    01  00     85.00
     MARTY   GRAW        TRAN STND RACK YUMMY FOODS IN          3766 8880 2323 0001
     TOTAL  100.00  85.00               01  00     85.00     15.00--


208  KING         100.00  99  00  00    01  00    100.00
     KATHY   CHRISSY     WALK STND RACK GLAMOUR HAIR C          4352 7554 4444 5822
     TOTAL  100.00 100.00               01  00    100.00      .00
```

**Report 6.1 (cont.)**

```
SULLKLIN INN          ROOM RATE REPORT 09/28/00(DOS DATE=01/06) 22:04  PAGE 02

                ROOM      FOLIO   BY  APP
ROOM  TYPE      RATE      RATE    ID  ID   REASON ADL CHILD   TODAY    VARIANCE

302  SUIT                200.00  01  00    00    01  00     200.00
       JOHN      SMITH            TRAN STND RACK
     TOTAL   200.00      200.00                  01  00     200.00       .00

303  KING                100.00  01  00    00    01  00     100.00
       TONY      TOURMALINE      TRAN STND RACK
     TOTAL   100.00      100.00                  01  00     100.00       .00

             1340.00    1335.00                            1335.00      5.00--


# OF ADULTS  -    0    1    2    3    4 OR MORE
                 ------------------------------------
# OF ROOMS -          12   1
(BEDDED ROOMS)

# OF ALLOCATED ROOMS -
```

**Report 6.1 (cont.)**

VARIANCE BY TARIFF TYPES  09/28/00

| TARIFF TYPE | RACK RATE | TODAY'S TOTAL | VARIANCE TOTAL | TARIFF TYPE | RACK RATE | TODAY'S TOTAL | VARIANCE TOTAL |
|---|---|---|---|---|---|---|---|
| RACK: | 1240.00 | 1250.00 | 10.00 | SPEC: | 100.00 | 85.00 | 15.00- |
| : | .00 | .00 | .00 | : | .00 | .00 | .00 |
| : | .00 | .00 | .00 | : | .00 | .00 | .00 |
| : | .00 | .00 | .00 | : | .00 | .00 | .00 |
| : | .00 | .00 | .00 | : | .00 | .00 | .00 |
| : | .00 | .00 | .00 | : | .00 | .00 | .00 |
| : | .00 | .00 | .00 | : | .00 | .00 | .00 |
| : | .00 | .00 | .00 | : | .00 | .00 | .00 |

**END OF REPORT**

**Report 6.2**

```
POSTINGS AUDIT REPORT (POSTINGS FOUND NOT CONNECTED TO FOLIOS)  09/28/00
ROOM #  POSITION ID    DATE    REF #   DESCRIPTION          AMOUNT

                                        TOTAL                  .00
END OF REPORT
```

**Report 6.3**

SULLKLIN INN          TRANSACTIONS  09/28/00 (DOS DATE=01/06) 22:07  PAGE 01

| REF# | AMOUNT | | TIME | ROOM | NAME | | ID | COMMENT/CC #/CITY LEDGER # |
|---|---|---|---|---|---|---|---|---|

ROOM

|  | 1335.00 | | | | SYSTEM POSTINGS | | | |

SUB TOTAL  1335.00


TAX

|  | 133.50 | | | | SYSTEM POSTINGS | | | |

SUB TOTAL  133.50


LOCAL TELE

| 123 | 1.20 | | 20:41 | 0201 | GRAW | MARTY | 01 | LOCAL |
| 2011 | 1.20 | XFER | 21:32 | 0200 | ADAMS | JOHN | 01 | LOCAL |
| 2001 | 1.20CR | XFER | 21:32 | 0201 | GRAW | MARTY | 01 | LOCAL |
| 1 | .50 | | 21:38 | 0201 | GRAW | MARTY | 01 | LOCAL |
| 2 | .50 | | 21:38 | 0201 | GRAW | MARTY | 01 | LOCAL |
| 3 | .50 | | 21:38 | 0201 | GRAW | MARTY | 01 | LOCAL |

SUB TOTAL  2.70


LONG DIST

| 852 | 15.00 | | 02:15 | 0103 | LEVY | ELI | 99 | LONDON |
| 756 | 18.00 | | 02:17 | 0108 | EUBUZZOFFSKYHAYWOOD | | 99 | PARIS FR |
| 1081 | 18.00 | XFER | 21:41 | 0103 | LEVY | ELI | 01 | PARIS FR |
| 1031 | 18.00CR | XFER | 21:41 | 0108 | EUBUZZOFFSKYHAYWOOD | | 01 | PARIS FR |

SUB TOTAL  33.00


FAX

| 505 | 5.00 | | 20:43 | 0201 | GRAW | MARTY | 01 | HOME |
| 505 | 1.00 | CORR | 21:30 | 0201 | GRAW | MARTY | 01 | ERROR |

SUB TOTAL  6.00


MOVIE

| 75 | 9.00 | | 02:16 | 0202 | WILLIAMS | LAUREN | CKO 99 | CLASSIC |
| 99 | 9.00 | | 15:23 | 0202 | WILLIAMS | LAUREN | CKO 99 | CLASSIC |
| 75 | 9.00CR | CORR | 21:41 | 0202 | WILLIAMS | LAUREN | CKO 01 | ERROR |

SUB TOTAL  9.00


CASH

|  | 110.00CR | | 15:18 | 0303 | TOURMALINE | TONY | 01 | |
| 201 | 100.00CR | | 20:44 | 0201 | GRAW | MARTY | 01 | CASH |

## Report 6.3 (cont.)

```
SULLKLIN INN         TRANSACTIONS  09/28/00 (DOS DATE=01/06) 22:07   PAGE 02

         REF#      AMOUNT    TIME    ROOM    NAME                    ID  COMMENT/CC #/CITY LEDGER #

            1     15.00CR   21:39   0103   LEVY       ELI           01  PD CASH

SUB TOTAL   225.00CR


CHECK
          101     50.00CR   20:45   0201   GRAW       MARTY         01  3766 8880 2323 0001

SUB TOTAL    50.00CR


AMEX
                 119.00CR   21:42   0202   WILLIAMS   LAUREN   CKO  01  3600 0090 0080 0067

SUB TOTAL   119.00CR


MAST
                 116.25CR   05:36   0303   THORNBERRY  ARNOLD  CKO  01  5400 0009 1313 1230
                  93.50CR   21:33   0204   COLM        DOTTIE  CKO  01  5468 1001 1000 1101

SUB TOTAL   209.75CR


END OF REPORT
```

**Report 6.3 (cont.)**

```
SULLKLIN INN        CORR/ADJUST/XFER 09/28/00(DOS DATE=01/06) 22 07 PAGE 01

    REF     TYPE         AMOUNT        TIME    ROOM   NAME                      ID  COMMENT


CORRECTIONS
    505    FAX          1.00   CORR   21:30    0201   GRAW      MARTY           01  ERROR
     75    MOVIE        9.00CR CORR   21:41    0202   WILLIAMS  LAUREN     CKO  01  ERROR

                        8.00CR TOTAL

ADJUSTMENTS

                         .00   TOTAL

TRANSFERS
   2011    LOCAL TELE   1.20   XFER   21:32    0200   ADAMS     JOHN            01  LOCAL
   2001    LOCAL TELE   1.20CR XFER   21:32    0201   GRAW      MARTY           01  LOCAL
   1081    LONG DIST    18.00  XFER   21:41    0103   LEVY      ELI             01  PARIS FR
   1031    LONG DIST    18.00CR XFER  21:41    0108   EUBUZZOFFSKYHAYWOOD       01  PARIS FR

                         .00   TOTAL

END OF REPORT
```

## Report 6.4

```
SULLKLIN INN        SUMMARY REVENUE REPORT   09/28/00  22 09    PAGE 01
GUEST LEDGER
```

| | GROSS | ADJUSTMENTS | CORRECTIONS | NET | ---- THIS YEAR ---- | |
|---|---|---|---|---|---|---|
| | | | | | MTD | YTD |
| **\*\*\* DEBITS \*\*\*** | | | | | | |
| ROOM | 1335.00 | .00 | .00 | 1335.00 | 2270.00 | 2270.00 |
| TAX | 133.50 | .00 | .00 | 133.50 | 227.00 | 227.00 |
| LOCAL TELE | 2.70 | .00 | .00 | 2.70 | 5.20 | 5.20 |
| LONG DIST | 33.00 | .00 | .00 | 33.00 | 51.50 | 51.50 |
| FAX | 5.00 | .00 | 1.00 | 6.00 | 35.25 | 35.25 |
| MOVIE | 18.00 | .00 | 9.00CR | 9.00 | 30.50 | 30.50 |
| ROOM ACCOUNT | .00 | .00 | .00 | .00 | .00 | .00 |
| REFUND | .00 | .00 | .00 | .00 | .00 | .00 |
| PAID OUT | .00 | .00 | .00 | .00 | .00 | .00 |
| TODAY'S DB | 1527.20 | .00 | 8.00CR | 1519.20 | 2619.45 | 2619.45 |
| **\*\*\* CREDITS \*\*\*** | | | | | | |
| CASH | 225.00CR | .00 | .00 | 225.00CR | 225.00CR | 225.00CR |
| CHECK | 50.00CR | .00 | .00 | 50.00CR | 50.00CR | 50.00CR |
| AMEX | 119.00CR | .00 | .00 | 119.00CR | 119.00CR | 119.00CR |
| VISA | .00 | .00 | .00 | .00 | .00 | .00 |
| MAST | 209.75CR | .00 | .00 | 209.75CR | 209.75CR | 209.75CR |
| DISC | .00 | .00 | .00 | .00 | .00 | .00 |
| D/B | .00 | .00 | .00 | .00 | .00 | .00 |
| ROOM ACCOUNT | .00 | .00 | .00 | .00 | .00 | .00 |
| APPLIED DEP | .00 | .00 | .00 | .00 | .00 | .00 |
| TODAY'S CR | 603.75CR | .00 | .00 | 603.75CR | 603.75CR | 603.75CR |
| TODAY'S DB. | 1527.20 | .00 | 8.00CR | 1519.20 | .00 | .00 |
| TODAY'S CR. | 603.75CR | .00 | .00 | 603.75CR | .00 | .00 |
| TODAY'S NET | 923.45 | .00 | 8.00CR | 915.45 | .00 | .00 |
| OPENING BAL | 1100.25 | .00 | .00 | 1100.25 | .00 | .00 |

**Report 6.4 (cont.)**

| | | | | | | |
|---|---|---|---|---|---|---|
| SYSTEM NET | 2023.70 | .00 | 8.00CR | 2015.70 | .00 | .00 |
| | | | | | | |
| SYS DEBITS | 2289.70 | .00 | 1.00 | 2290.70 | .00 | .00 |
| SYS CREDITS | 275.00CR | .00 | .00 | 275.00CR | .00 | .00 |
| SYSTEM NET | 2014.70 | .00 | 1.00 | 2015.70 | .00 | .00 |

**Report 6.5**

```
SULLKLIN INN       CHECK OUTS FOR 09/28/00 (DOS DATE=01/06)    PAGE 01

-------------- FOLIO #: 0927-0004 --------------
COLM       DOTTIE
 1001 HYPERTEXT WAY
 SAN JOSE, CA
                    95112
 408555-0101
GUEST TYPE: WALK   SEGMENT: SPEC
HISTORY NUMBERS:
COMMENTS:
ROOM: 204 - NIGHTS: 1 CHECK-OUT TIME: 21:33  BY I.D.: 01
PAYMENT BY MS - CREDIT CARD #: 5468 1001 1000 1101
RATE HISTORY:
 85.00 FOR  1 NIGHT(S)
  1.  09/27     1  ROOM           85.00    SYSTEM
  2.  09/27        TAX             8.50    SYSTEM
  3.  09/28        MAST           93.50CR  01
                   *** BALANCE ***   .00

-------------- FOLIO #: 0927-0007 --------------
THORNBERRY  ARNOLD
 1313 MOCKINGBIRD LANE
 BALTIMORE, MD                              COM:  HARMLESS MEDICAL PRODUCTS
                    21218
 410555-1313
GUEST TYPE: TRAN   SEGMENT: STND
HISTORY NUMBERS:
COMMENTS:
ROOM: 303 - NIGHTS: 1 CHECK-OUT TIME: 05:36  BY I.D.: 01
PAYMENT BY MS - CREDIT CARD #: 5400 0009 1313 1230
RATE HISTORY:
 100.00 FOR  1 NIGHT(S)
  1.  09/27     1  ROOM          100.00    SYSTEM
  2.  09/27        TAX            10.00    SYSTEM
  3.  09/27     1  LOCAL TELE       .50    99
  4.  09/27     2  LOCAL TELE       .50    99
  5.  09/27     4  FAX             5.25    99
  6.  09/28        MAST          116.25CR  01
                   *** BALANCE ***   .00

-------------- FOLIO #: 0927-0009 --------------
WILLIAMS    LAUREN
 154 STONE LANE
 ORLANDO, FL
                    32824
 407555-1777
GUEST TYPE: WALK   SEGMENT: STND
HISTORY NUMBERS:
COMMENTS:
ROOM: 202 - NIGHTS: 1 CHECK-OUT TIME: 21:42  BY I.D.: 01
PAYMENT BY AX - CREDIT CARD #: 3600 0090 0080 0067
RATE HISTORY:
 100.00 FOR  1 NIGHT(S)
  1.  09/27     1  ROOM          100.00    SYSTEM
  2.  09/27        TAX            10.00    SYSTEM
  3.  09/28    75  MOVIE           9.00    99 *
  4.  09/28    99  MOVIE           9.00    99
  5.  09/28    75  MOVIE    CORR   9.00CR  01 *
```

**Report 6.5 (cont.)**

```
SULLKLIN INN       CHECK OUTS FOR 09/28/00 (DOS DATE=01/06)   PAGE 02
6.   09/28         AMEX                119.00CR   01
                   *** BALANCE ***         .00


GRAND TOTAL FOR ALL FOLIOS =         .00



END OF CHECK OUT LIST
```

## Report 6.6

```
SULLKLIN INN         NO SHOW FOR 09/28/00    PAGE 01

----------
  1. MANIFEST    MRS   NAN         CONF.#: 00000654  ID: 99
     GTD TRAN  STND  RACK  ARRIVE: 09/28/00  DEPART: 09/29/00  RESV. MADE: 09/27
     1 KING   1 PER    1 NIGHTS   100.00
     2 SOUTH NAAMANS RD
     WILMINGTON, DE
                         19808
  CC#: 3663 4576 5476 5677         PHONE #: 302555-7890
  COMMENTS: LATE ARRIVAL
  HIST: N  #: 0000  0000  0000
----------
  2. MURKY      MR    PETER        CONF.#: 00000664  ID: 01
     GTD TRAN  STND  RACK  ARRIVE: 09/28/00  DEPART: 09/29/00  RESV. MADE: 09/28
     1 DD    1 PER    1 NIGHTS    75.00
     999 RAINFOREST ROAD                        COM: PRECISION DATA COLLECTION
     PORTLAND, OR
                         97206
  CC#: 3747 9999 9511 1159         PHONE #: 503555-9999
  HIST: N  #: 0000  0000  0000
----------
END OF REPORT
```

**Report 6.6 (cont.)**

```
SULLKLIN INN          CANCELLATIONS OF 09/28/00  (DOS DATE=01/06)    PAGE 01


    ----------
ANULARA      LEE           CONF.#: 0000064D  ID: 99
  ARRIVAL DATE - 09/29/00  GTD
  1 DD     1 PER   10 NIGHTS    85.00

  1776 RIOS RD
  SAN DIEGO, CA
                  92130
  CREDIT CARD #: 6577 7896 9000 0900
  COMMENTS: REQ RM ON 1ST FL
          CANCELLATION #:   30928   ID: 01   REASON: 01
          CANCELLED BY: SELF
    ----------
END OF CANCELLATION REPORT
```

**Report 6.7**

```
SULLKLIN INN        COMP ROOM REPORT FOR 09/28/00  (DOS DATE=01/06)

ROOM  ROOM         NAME            COMPANY              GROUP            GUEST TYPE
NO.   TYPE


END OF COMP ROOM REPORT
```

**Report 6.8**

```
SULLKLIN INN          DEPOSITS FOR 09/28/00  (DOS DATE=01/06)  TIME: 22:13  PAGE 01


MAY         APRIL            # 0000064C    ID:01 TOT DEP$    110.00 09/28/00
   ARRIVAL DATE 04/28/01  GTD
   1 KING   1  PER    5 NIGHTS    100.00

   900 SPRING GARDEN ST
   PHILADELPHIA, PA
                   19811
   COMMENTS: WILL MAIL DEPOSIT
        TODAY'S ACTIVITY:    01  CK     110.00 ADDED      SUB-TOTAL    110.00 ADDED
---------------------
PROUD       HARRIS           # 00000652    ID:01 TOT DEP$    110.00 09/28/00
   ARRIVAL DATE 05/27/01  GTD
   1 KING   2  PER    5 NIGHTS    100.00

   8571 TALBOT RD
   BLUE BELL, PA
                   19422
        TODAY'S ACTIVITY:    01  CK     110.00 ADDED      SUB-TOTAL    110.00 ADDED
---------------------
DEPOSITS ADDED TODAY        220.00
DEPOSIT SUBTRACTED TODAY        .00 (INCLUDES DEPOSITS CANCELLED TODAY)
TODAY'S NET                 220.00 ADDED


          ****** HIGHLIGHTED LINES MAY BE A COMBINATION OF SEVERAL ENTRIES
                 FOR ONE OR MORE OPERATOR ID#'s AND/OR PAYMENT TYPES


SULLKLIN INN          CANCELLED DEPOSITS 09/28/00  (DOS DATE=01/06)  TIME: 22:14  PAGE 01


                              DEPOSIT TOTAL = $       .00


SULLKLIN INN          NO-SHOW DEPOSITS 09/28/00  (DOS DATE=01/06)  TIME: 22:14  PAGE 01


                              DEPOSIT TOTAL = $       .00


          ****** PLEASE NOTE THAT ANY DEPOSITS FOR NO-SHOW RESERVATIONS
                 WILL BE DELETED DURING THE NIGHT AUDIT 'Z'


SULLKLIN INN          APPLIED DEPOSITS 09/28/00  (DOS DATE=01/06)  TIME: 22:14  PAGE 01


                              DEPOSIT TOTAL = $       .00
END OF REPORT
```

**Report 6.8 (cont.)**

```
SULLKLIN INN          RESV. FILE DEPOSITS 09/28/00  (DOS DATE=01/06)  TIME: 22:16  PAGE 01

                          ADVANCE DEPOSITS BY ARRIVAL DATE

ARR DATE     CONF#     GUEST/GROUP           NIGHTS    DEP AMT   DATE RECD    ID
04/28/01   #0000064C   MAY        APRIL        5       110.00   09/28/00     01
05/27/01   #00000652   PROUD      HARRIS       5       110.00   09/28/00     01
                          TOTAL DEPOSITS LISTED = $     220.00
END OF REPORT
```

**Report 6.8 (cont.)**

SULLKLIN INN          OVERDUE DEPOSITS AS OF 09/28/00  (DOS DATE=01/06)  TIME: 22:17  PAGE 01


                                    DEPOSITS OUTSTANDING = $        .00
END OF REPORT

## Report 6.9

```
SULLKLIN INN          BUILDING MAINTENANCE REPORT 09/28/00 (DOS DATE=01/06) 22:18

                  IN              DONE
 WO#   ROOM   TIME    DATE    TIME    DATE    DESCRIPTION


   1    200   21:48 09/28/00  21:48 09/28/00  REPAIR SINK

   2    201   21:54 09/28/00                  REMOTE CONTROL NOT OWRKING

END OF REPORT
```

**Report 6.10**

```
SULLKLIN INN         DAILY MESSAGE REPORT   09/28/00 (DOS DATE=01/06) 22:19 PAGE 01


   1 RM: 104-1 09/27/00   TAKEN BY: 99
CALL THE OFFICE

   2 RM: 303-1 09/27/00   TAKEN BY: 99
CALL GINGER JONES AT 215-555-9998
***** THIS GUEST CHECKED-OUT TODAY ********

   3 RM: 303-1 09/27/00   TAKEN BY: 99
MIKE WILL MEET YOU AT CHEZ NOUS RESTAURANT AT 8 PM DRESS CASUAL
***** THIS GUEST CHECKED-OUT TODAY ********

   4 RM: 100-1 IN: 21:51  TAKEN BY: 01  DELIVERED  DEL. BY: 01 AT 21:51
CALL OFFICE AT 999-0909

   5 RM: 208-1 IN: 21:55  TAKEN BY: 01
CALL SHOP ASAP

   6 RM: 108-1 IN: 21:56  TAKEN BY: 01
PLEASE CALL YOUR MOTHER WHEN YOU GET IN

END OF MESSAGE REPORT
```

**Report 6.10 (cont.)**

```
                        M E S S A G E
                        --------------

ROOM NUMBER:  104    NAME: JAVED     MUHAMMADI


MESSAGE RECEIVED ON 09/27/00 AT 22:33  BY CLERK NUMBER: 99



CALL THE OFFICE
```

**Report 6.10 (cont.)**

```
                    M E S S A G E
                    --------------


ROOM NUMBER:  208    NAME: KATHY    CHRISSY


MESSAGE RECEIVED ON 09/28/00 AT 21:55  BY CLERK NUMBER: 01



CALL SHOP ASAP
```

**Report 6.10 (cont.)**

```
                    M E S S A G E
                    --------------

ROOM NUMBER:  108    NAME: HAYWOOD   EUBUZZOFFSKY


MESSAGE RECEIVED ON 09/28/00 AT 21:56  BY CLERK NUMBER: 01



PLEASE CALL YOUR MOTHER WHEN YOU GET IN

END OF REPORT
```

# Report 6.11

```
SULLKLIN INN        FINAL SUMMARY REVENUE REPORT   09/28/00  22 21    PAGE 01
GUEST LEDGER
                                                           ---- THIS YEAR ----
                GROSS    ADJUSTMENTS   CORRECTIONS    NET      MTD        YTD
*** DEBITS ***
```

| | GROSS | ADJUSTMENTS | CORRECTIONS | NET | MTD | YTD |
|---|---|---|---|---|---|---|
| **\*\*\* DEBITS \*\*\*** | | | | | | |
| ROOM | 1335.00 | .00 | .00 | 1335.00 | 2270.00 | 2270.00 |
| TAX | 133.50 | .00 | .00 | 133.50 | 227.00 | 227.00 |
| LOCAL TELE | 2.70 | .00 | .00 | 2.70 | 5.20 | 5.20 |
| LONG DIST | 33.00 | .00 | .00 | 33.00 | 51.50 | 51.50 |
| FAX | 5.00 | .00 | 1.00 | 6.00 | 35.25 | 35.25 |
| MOVIE | 18.00 | .00 | 9.00CR | 9.00 | 30.50 | 30.50 |
| ROOM ACCOUNT | .00 | .00 | .00 | .00 | .00 | .00 |
| REFUND | .00 | .00 | .00 | .00 | .00 | .00 |
| PAID OUT | .00 | .00 | .00 | .00 | .00 | .00 |
| TODAY'S DB | 1527.20 | .00 | 8.00CR | 1519.20 | 2619.45 | 2619.45 |
| **\*\*\* CREDITS \*\*\*** | | | | | | |
| CASH | 225.00CR | .00 | .00 | 225.00CR | 225.00CR | 225.00CR |
| CHECK | 50.00CR | .00 | .00 | 50.00CR | 50.00CR | 50.00CR |
| AMEX | 119.00CR | .00 | .00 | 119.00CR | 119.00CR | 119.00CR |
| VISA | .00 | .00 | .00 | .00 | .00 | .00 |
| MAST | 209.75CR | .00 | .00 | 209.75CR | 209.75CR | 209.75CR |
| DISC | .00 | .00 | .00 | .00 | .00 | .00 |
| D/B | .00 | .00 | .00 | .00 | .00 | .00 |
| ROOM ACCOUNT | .00 | .00 | .00 | .00 | .00 | .00 |
| APPLIED DEP | .00 | .00 | .00 | .00 | .00 | .00 |
| TODAY'S CR | 603.75CR | .00 | .00 | 603.75CR | 603.75CR | 603.75CR |
| TODAY'S DB. | 1527.20 | .00 | 8.00CR | 1519.20 | .00 | .00 |
| TODAY'S CR. | 603.75CR | .00 | .00 | 603.75CR | .00 | .00 |
| TODAY'S NET | 923.45 | .00 | 8.00CR | 915.45 | .00 | .00 |
| OPENING BAL | 1100.25 | .00 | .00 | 1100.25 | .00 | .00 |

**Report 6.11 (cont.)**

| | | | | | | |
|---|---|---|---|---|---|---|
| SYSTEM NET | 2023.70 | .00 | 8.00CR | 2015.70 | .00 | .00 |
| | | | | | | |
| SYS DEBITS | 2289.70 | .00 | 1.00 | 2290.70 | .00 | .00 |
| SYS CREDITS | 275.00CR | .00 | .00 | 275.00CR | .00 | .00 |
| SYSTEM NET | 2014.70 | .00 | 1.00 | 2015.70 | .00 | .00 |

## Report 6.11 (cont.)

```
SULLKLIN INN        OCCUPANCY DAY END SUMMARY   09/28/00 (DOS DATE=01/06) 22:21

            TOTAL      TODAY    MONTH TO DATE    YEAR TO DATE

DD           11       4 036%       7 021%          7 021%
KING         11       8 073%      15 042%         15 042%
SUIT          3       1 033%       1 017%          1 017%

TOTALS       25      13 052%      23 031%         23 031%



****  AVERAGE ROOM RATES  ****

ROOM NIGHTS          13             23               23
$ REVENUE       1335.00        1335.00          1335.00
AVERAGE RATE     102.69          58.04            58.04

END OF REPORT
```

**Report 6.11 (cont.)**

SULLKLIN INN          CREDIT CARD TRANSFERS TO A/R CREDIT CARD ACCOUNTS 09/28/00

**Report 6.11 (cont.)**

```
SULLKLIN INN           ACCOUNTS RECEIVABLE TRANSFERS FOR 09/28/00


TOTAL A/R TRANSFERRED TODAY = $           .00CR

TOTAL A/R CHECKED OUT TODAY = $           .00CR

*** THESE TWO FIGURES SHOULD BE EQUAL ***


END OF ACCOUNTS RECEIVABLE TRANSFERS
```

**Report 6.11 (cont.)**

```
         A/R POSTINGS REPORT  09/28/00  (DOS DATE=01/06)    22:21      PAGE 01

    REF#      AMOUNT    ID  TYPE       ACCOUNT

END OF REPORT
```

# Report 6.11 (cont.)

```
SULLKLIN INN      FINAL SUMMARY REVENUE REPORT  09/28/00  (DOS DATE=01/06)    22:21 PAGE 01
A/R - CITY LEDGER

                GROSS    CORRECTIONS     NET
** DEBITS **


ROOM            .00        .00          .00

TAX             .00        .00          .00

LOCAL TELE      .00        .00          .00

LONG DIST       .00        .00          .00

FAX             .00        .00          .00

MOVIE           .00        .00          .00

ROOM ACCOUNT    .00        .00          .00

REFUND          .00        .00          .00

PAID OUT        .00        .00          .00


TODAY'S DB      .00        .00          .00


** CREDITS **


CASH            .00        .00          .00

CHECK           .00        .00          .00

AMEX            .00        .00          .00

VISA            .00        .00          .00

MAST            .00        .00          .00

DISC            .00        .00          .00

D/B             .00        .00          .00

ROOM ACCOUNT    .00        .00          .00

APPLIED DEP     .00        .00          .00


TODAY'S CR      .00        .00          .00


TODAY'S DB.     .00        .00          .00
TODAY'S CR.     .00        .00          .00
TODAY'S NET     .00        .00          .00
OPENING BAL     .00        .00          .00
SYSTEM NET      .00        .00          .00
```

**Report 6.11 (cont.)**

```
*** NOTE: TODAY'S OPENING BALANCE SHOULD EQUAL YESTERDAY'S SYSTEM NET ***
```

**Report 6.11 (cont.)**

```
NET OUTSTANDING BALANCE      09/28/00

ADVANCED DEPOSITS OUTSTANDING

OPENING BALANCE          .00
DEPOSITS ADDED         220.00
                               DEPOSITS RETURNED        .00   (INCLUDES DEPOSITS CANCELLED TODAY)
                               NO SHOW DEPOSITS         .00
                               DEPOSITS APPLIED         .00
TOTAL SUBTRACTED       .00CR
SYSTEM NET             220.00



NET OUTSTANDING BALANCE

    GUEST LEDGER BALANCE         2015.70
  + A/R CITY LEDGER BALANCE          .00
  - ADVANCED DEPOSITS OUTSTANDING   220.00
                                 ---------
  = NET OUTSTANDING BALANCE        1795.70
```

# Notes

**Notes**

**Notes**

**Notes**

**Notes**

**Notes**

**Notes**

**Notes**